CHIVAL

From Myths to Facts

Diego Beltrutti di San Biagio

CHIVALRY AND MASONRY – FROM MYTHS TO FACTS.

ISBN: 978-1-917613-31-6

www.sanctisepulchri.com

Email: sanctisepulchri@gmail.com

First English edition: July 2024

This text is based on the book 'Cavaliere e Massone: analisi di un binomio controverso' of the same author.

The crown of victory is promised only to those who fight.

Table of Contents

Presentation

What is the significance today of contributing to the editing of a research on spiritual knighthood when, in recent years, research and publications on the theme of 'chivalry' have become increasingly abundant? It must be acknowledged, however, that in this field, alongside excellent research, there is no shortage of subpar works, superficial if not outright trivial.

Those engaged in 'neo-Templarism' are well aware of the numerous texts that are not independent but written to attract attention, blatantly promoting a specific agenda; the available bibliography is also heavily influenced by aligned authors.

While essays from the exoteric, initiatic, and masonic realms are readily available, texts that propose the authentic values of spiritual chivalry in this post-modern, secularized, and self-referential world are hard to find. Thus, this publication aims to be a clear and balanced guide with defined contours for those intending to follow the traditional chivalric path, particularly the Christian one.

With this goal in mind, we have endeavoured to highlight the peculiarities and differences existing between a knight militant in a Christian order and an individual who has joined chivalric organizations within Freemasonry.

The attempts made by the Catholic Church over the last three centuries to protect itself and its chivalric orders from Masonic infiltrations do not appear to have achieved the desired results. The Anglo-Saxon world, especially within certain lobbies, pushes in another direction, both on this side and beyond the Atlantic.

During the recent coronation of King Charles III, as monarch of the United Kingdom of Great Britain and Northern Ireland, we observed that the king holds the position of the supreme leader of the Anglican Protestant Church and Grand Master of the United Lodge of England simultaneously.

The ceremony highlighted how, beyond the Channel, the Anglican Church and Freemasonry go hand in hand, and how the English crown intends to play a role not only in the West but also in the Near East. Was it perhaps a coincidence that Byzantine litanies resonated in the cathedral?

Given that the Catholic Church, since the time of Pope Clement V, distanced itself from the chivalric order that had achieved so much in the defence of Christianity, it is not surprising that today a certain number of individuals eager to serve in spiritual chivalry find themselves co-opted by Masonic lodges. This situation may be related to, and perhaps even a consequence of, the fact that beyond the Tiber, anything resembling a 'chivalric order' is viewed with extreme circumspection and distrust.

The Sovereign Military Order of Malta and the Equestrian Order of the Holy Sepulcher of Jerusalem continue to be the only chivalric and equestrian orders recognized by the Holy See.

To the question, «Is there a Freemasonry problem in chivalric and equestrian orders?» it's not easy to answer. It is known that there are orders of chivalry not acknowledged by the Catholic Church, as they are seen as expressions of the high degrees of Freemasonry. However, providing a numerical dimension to the Freemasons belonging to the orders recognized by the Holy See is more challenging.

Popular wisdom states, in a very picturesque way, that 'throwing the baby out with the bathwater' is never an acceptable solution. On the other hand, Matthew (13, 24-30) reminds us how the weeds must be separated from the wheat. Yet, in reference to the orders of chivalry, it seems that this operation of discerning the children of light from the children of darkness is not possible, perhaps even unwanted.

Even if today the world of chivalry appears to most as a historical niche, an enclave, a world confined and reserved for lovers of medieval tradition, there is great excitement around this ancient Christian institution, and many people declare themselves eager to become part of it. With these assumptions, it seemed useful to us to clarify this controversial issue by providing the reader with useful cultural tools to reflect, in an independent and preconception-free manner, on two different chivalric paths: the Christian and the Masonic ones.

The author hopes that the Congregation for the Doctrine of the Faith, after having pronounced itself on the dual membership of Catholics, can express itself, with an innovative and merciful vision, also on those chivalric groups which, not being linked to

Freemasonry, not aiming at the reconstitution of the Order of the Temple, and not being members of recognized orders, however, represent the expression of a strong and genuine desire to serve Christianity.

Introduction

The analysis of the existing relationships between Spiritual Chivalry and Freemasonry requires a free and sincere reflection. Therefore, it is necessary to agree on the historical value to be given to documented and/or mythical and legendary realities. It must be established whether these two ways of evaluating, reading, and commenting on historical events are equivalent or carry different weights.

It is known that myths do not represent specific events and do not narrate certain, historically datable facts. They reflect the culture, fears, and expectations of the peoples that produced them; these stories are not based on reliable sources but are a fanciful, dreamlike representation.

Analyzing myths, we realize that they have tried to explain events that may have happened in a distant past or that are believed to have happened in that way and at that time, but for which there is no concrete, tangible evidence.

> It is extremely fascinating to want to see, at the origin of Freemasonry, within myths, Templars, Rosicrucians, and others, but one must separate myth from history. And, before these can intersect again, one must go through history. At the moment, there is no

> documentary evidence attesting to the Templars as the founders of Freemasonry. Returning to the history of ideas, symbolism, and myth, there is a reversal of perspective. Freemasonry has appropriated the Templars and the 'values' of the Templars[1].

A fact is certain; on March 22, 1312, with the bull *Vox in Excelso*, Pope Clement V suppressed the Order of the Temple by virtue of his papal authority, through an administrative decision rather than as a result of a condemnation[2].

> [...] Now, it is true that from the trials conducted against this Order, it cannot canonically be declared heretical with a definitive sentence. However, due to the heresies attributed to it, the Order itself has gained a terrible reputation. Many of its members, including the Grand Master, the visitor of France, and the most prominent priors, through their voluntary confessions regarding these heresies, have been convicted of errors and crimes. Furthermore, these

---

[1] "Symbology of Templar Chivalry and Freemasonry, Conference: Templars in Casale Monferrato and Surroundings, April 19, 2015, Leone M., December 2, 2015. URL: *https://micheleleone.it/simbolismo-templare-cavalleresco-e-massonico/* (*Verified 23/09/2022*).

[2] *Vox in Excelso*. Url: *https//it.cathopedia.org/wiki/vox_in_excelso/ (Verified 05/04/2022).*

confessions make this Order very suspicious, and this infamy and mistrust make it downright abominable and hateful to the Holy Church of God, its prelates, its kings, Christian princes, and other Catholics.

Moreover, it can reasonably be believed that from now on, no one would be willing to enter this Order, and therefore it would become useless to the Church of God and to the continuation of the mission of the Holy Land, to which it had been dedicated.

Since from the postponement of the decision, that is, from the resolution of this matter - for the definition and promulgation of which a deadline in the present council had been assigned by us for the friars of this Order - there would follow the total loss, distribution, and squandering of the assets of the Temple, which have long been offered, bound, granted by the faithful of Christ to aid the Holy Land in fighting the enemies of the Christian faith; considering that, according to some, the sentence of condemnation against the Order of the Templars for their crimes should be immediately promulgated, and according to others, based on the trials already conducted against the same Order, a sentence of condemnation could not be issued, we, after long and mature reflection, with only God before our eyes and looking solely at the utility of the Holy Land, without leaning either to the right or to the left, deemed it appropriate to choose the path of decision and resolution, through which scandals will be removed, dangers will be avoided, and assets in aid of the Holy Land will be preserved.

The infamy, suspicion, sensational reports, and all the other things already mentioned, all against the Order, and furthermore, the hidden and clandestine admission of the friars of the same Order, the difference in the behaviour, way of life, and customs of many of those friars from those of other Christians - especially the fact that by admitting new members, they obliged them not to reveal the manner of their admission and not to leave the Order - lead to presumptions against them. Reflecting, moreover, that all this has given rise to a serious scandal against this Order, which could hardly be silenced if the Order continued to exist, and considering the dangers to faith and souls, and the numerous heinous misdeeds of the majority of the friars of the same Order, and many other just reasons and causes, we have had to resolve to the following decisions.

The majority of the cardinals, and at least four-fifths of those elected by the entire council, deemed it more fitting, advantageous, and useful for the honour of God, the preservation of the Christian faith, aid to the Holy Land, and many other just reasons, that the path of a measure by the apostolic see be followed instead. This measure involves suspending the Order from all functions and assigning the assets to the use for which they were intended. It also

> provides for the salutary care of the persons of the same Order, rather than the path of respecting the right to defence and the extension of this issue. Even in other cases, albeit without fault of the friars, the Church of Rome has sometimes suppressed orders of far greater importance for reasons incomparably more modest than those mentioned.
>
> Therefore, with bitterness and sorrow, we decree that: not with a definitive sentence, but with an apostolic measure, we, with the approval of the Holy Council, suspend the Order of the Templars from all functions, its rule, its attire, and its name, by absolute, perpetual decree, prohibiting it forever and severely forbidding anyone thereafter to enter it, assume its attire, wear it, or intend to behave as a Templar. If anyone acts to the contrary, they shall incur the sentence of excommunication *ipso facto*.

Even though the King of France, Philip IV, known as 'The Fair,' on March 18, 1314, closed the Templar case with the death by burning of Jacques de Molay, the 23rd and last Grand Master of the Order, and the Catholic Church contributed to putting an end to this institution by the will of Pope Clement V, in today's society, there continues to be great interest in chivalry, especially the Templar chivalry.

Understanding the reasons for this interest is not easy. The phenomenon can be explained by the desire,

Let us remember Matthew (5, 37): «*Let your 'Yes' be 'Yes,' and your 'No,' 'No.' For whatever is more than these is from the evil one*». From this passage, we understand that the thought of the Christian must be clear, transparent, and free from shades of gray.

> The Church is uncompromising on principles because it believes, but it is tolerant in practice because it loves; the enemies of the Church are tolerant in principles because they do not believe, but uncompromising in practice because they do not love. The Church absolves sinners, the enemies of the Church absolve sins[3].

The fact that Freemasonry has undergone so many excommunications from the Catholic Church might lead to the idea of persecution towards this institution. In reality, there has never been relentlessness. The issue is that the Catholic Church and Freemasonry present absolutely different attitudes towards evil and those who commit it. Charity, love, tolerance, mercy, and truth are concepts elaborated in a different way by the two organizations.

John (10, 11) expresses it this way: «*I am the good shepherd. The good shepherd gives His life for the sheep*». Chivalry requires clarity of behaviour. You cannot have one foot in two stirrups. You cannot be of

---

[3] Garrigou-Lagrange R., 1923, *Dieu: son existence et sa nature solution Thomiste des Antinomes Agnostiques,* Paris, France, Gabriel Beauchesne, p. 725.

the light and also of the darkness. You have to choose. Either you are with the wolves or with the lambs. That's why, if you are a knight of Christ, a knight of the light, you cannot simultaneously be a knight of the darkness.

Since we have been granted the use of our free will, Masons, like any other individual, are free to follow their own path. But for knights of an order with ancient and solid Christian foundations to ask to enter Freemasonry, to belong to an organization that works against the Church of which they are a part, seems decidedly too much. In these cases, perhaps, there would be a need for a psychologist or psychoanalyst to delve into the depths to understand why such an idea might cross someone's mind. To lead to excommunication, to create a paradoxical ecclesial situation, are the choices of individuals. Whether it is a Mason asking to enter a declaredly Catholic chivalric order or a Catholic being censured for a probable entry into Freemasonry, the situation is paradoxical. It is the individual, with their own free and autonomous choices, who puts themselves in an untenable position, which, for the Christian, entails the loss of some fundamental rights, such as access to the sacraments.

Remember that the state of ‘excommunication’ does not imply that someone authorized will come to the Church to pick up that person and then throw them out; someone who has been ‘excommunicated’ continues to be a Christian forever because baptism makes them so, and baptism is irreversible. However, as mentioned above, they will be a Christian with fewer rights because, for example, they cannot approach the Eucharist.

Referring briefly to excommunications, it is worth remembering that Masons were excommunicated for the first time on April 28, 1738, when Pope Clement XII issued the apostolic letter *In Eminenti Apostulatus Specula*[4]. The excommunication was reiterated on May 18, 1751, by Pope Benedict XIV with the bull *Providas Romanorum Pontificum*[5]. Several other excommunications followed these two.

In the fall of 1980, the 'Declaration of the German Bishops' Conference' regarding the membership of Catholics in Freemasonry was made public. This document, detailed and in-depth, was drawn up by members of a bilateral commission, consisting of representatives from German lodges and prelates of the Catholic Church. After six years of meetings and investigations, the document concluded with the Church's exclusion of any possibility of dual membership.

On November 26, 1983, the Congregation for the Doctrine of the Faith issued a declaration on Masonic associations, reaffirming the incompatibility between the Christian faith and Freemasonry.

Historical events and documents confirm that spiritual chivalry has always been linked to the Church of Rome since its constitution. Nevertheless, within Masonic circles, a different narrative is popular.

---

[4] "In the Eminent Seat of the Apostolate".

[5] "The Provident (laws) of the Roman Pontiffs."

In an attempt to delve into this narrative, I would like to mention the conference 'Il Cuore e la Spada. L'Ora delle Scelte[6]' held in August 2015 in Castignano (AP) and organized by the Circumscriptional College of the Worshipful Masters of the Marche.

Stefano Bisi, at that time the Grand Master of the Grand Orient of Italy (G.·.O.·.I.·.), was present at the conference[7]. Among the speakers representing the Masonic component within chivalry were Paolo Corallini and Fabrizio Bartoli, respectively Grand Prior and High Dignitary of the Templars O.S.M.T.H.[8]

From this meeting, it was evident that the historical connection between Freemasonry and the Order of the Temple is a divisive topic, even within Freemasonry itself. Not all Masons accept the tradition that some knights, surviving the trial in Paris, would have left France, crossed the English Channel, and joined Robert Bruce's army in Scotland. Subsequently, after laying down their arms, they would have joined the guilds of the builders and from there entered Freemasonry.

There is another version regarding the origin of the Templar component of Freemasonry. The presence of Templar degrees would be inspired by the action of

---

6 "The Heart and The Sword. The Hour of Choices".

7 "The Grand Orient of Italy is the oldest Masonic institution in Italy."

8 The 'Ordo Supremus Militaris Templi Hierosolymitani' or O.S.M.T.H. (Sovereign Military Order of the Temple of Jerusalem) is an association not recognized by the Holy See, being of a neo-Templar origin and having a Christian ecumenical vision, within whose ranks Masonic brothers operate.

writer and philosopher Andrew Michael Ramsay. In December 1736, he delivered a famous oration in a Paris lodge where he defined Freemasonry as the heir of chivalric orders.

Ramsay, after arriving in Rome and becoming the tutor to the children of the *Old Pretender*[9] to the English crown, made a significant effort to persuade Cardinal de Fleury and eventually Pope Clement XII of the merit of his project. The goal was to restore a Catholic king to the throne of England with the mediation and assistance of Freemasonry. The outcome of this initiative was not as hoped; in fact, the Pope did not appreciate the idea and denounced Freemasonry.

In the mentioned conference, Corallini presented his research titled 'Freemasons and Templars: Ancient Brothers?' emphasizing the claim that the Templars had excavated undisturbed under the Temple of Jerusalem for years. Consequently, they would have returned to Europe with important relics and a vast wealth of knowledge.

Corallini and Bartoli expressed certainty about the existence of irrefutable evidence, suggesting the presence of Templar knights in Scotland and their involvement in the establishment of the Kilwilling Lodge, considered the 'Zero Lodge'. However, what they assert corresponds more to their personal desire to bestow noble origins upon Freemasonry than to the existence of documents and concrete evidence. In fact, there is no documentary evidence supporting the thesis

---

[9] James Francis Edward Stuart, known as the 'Old Pretender,' was the son of King James II and Mary of Modena.

that medieval chivalry had a second, well-camouflaged soul, expressing a secret adherence to the values of the Freemasonry.

Nevertheless, their assertions seem to align more with a personal desire to give noble origins to Freemasonry than with the existence of concrete documents and evidence. Indeed, there is no documentary evidence in favour of the thesis that medieval chivalry had a second, well-camouflaged soul, expressing a secret adherence to the values of the Free Masonry.

The thoughts of Alain Demurger, a historian, medievalist, and professor at the Sorbonne, leave no doubt about it:

> Together with the Cathars and Joan of Arc, the Templars fuel one of the inexhaustible veins of that pseudo-history whose sole purpose is to offer eager readers their ration of mysteries and secrets...[10]

If this had happened, this organization could no longer have been called the 'Knights of the Temple,' as adherence to the creed of Freemasonry would have made it incompatible with belonging to the 'Militia of Christ.' The fact that there are now associations calling themselves 'Orders,' even without the historical

---

[10] Alain Demurger, 1987, *Vita e morte dell'ordine dei Templari*, Milano, Italia, Garzanti.

requirements to claim such an honour; the fact that these associations often declare a direct descent from the Order of the Temple, knowing that the Order of the Temple was suppressed in 1312; the fact that there are Masonic lodges that accept among their affiliates anticlerical, gnostic, agnostic, or even atheist individuals... all of this helps us understand the historical confusion and ambiguity that reigns in the majority of groups calling themselves chivalrous.

The Italian state sought to remedy the casual use of membership in chivalric orders, and it did so in the distant year of 1951 with Law 178, which is still in force. Beyond considerations that could be made about dynastic orders and those of merit linked to the House of Savoy, it seems evident that, with the monarchy gone, the Italian Republic wanted to regulate the matter in a way quite different from what was previously in place.

The teaching from the reading of Law 178 is that in Italy, individuals can bear honours or chivalric distinctions conferred by non-national orders or foreign states *only with prior authorization by the President of the Republic, upon the proposal of the Minister of Foreign Affairs (M.A.E.).*

The use of honours from the Holy See, the Order of Malta, and the Equestrian Order of the Holy Sepulchre is allowed due to an agreement between the State and the Catholic Church. Article 8 further states that entities, associations, or individuals cannot confer honours, decorations, or chivalric distinctions, and individuals cannot use them. This last case applies to the majority of so-called 'Templar orders,' which, in reality, are not orders due to a lack of documented historical basis but are typically associations formed in recent years. This includes, among others, chivalric orders forming part of the higher degrees of the Ancient and Accepted Scottish Rite.

In addition to reasons related to the medieval suppression of the Templar order, which explains why the Holy See does not grant churches for equestrian investitures, there is also the fact that the vast majority, if not all, of the 'chivalric orders' or 'Templar orders' active in Italy, besides being associated with Freemasonry and therefore unwelcome, are not recognized by the Italian Republic, considering them illegal. Dual membership, i.e., simultaneous membership in chivalry and Freemasonry, is not only prohibited by the Church but also deemed nonsensical. However, there is a minimal transfer from the Catholic world to Freemasonry today.

Simultaneously, many Freemasons express a desire to embark on the chivalric path. Understanding the reasons behind these behaviours is not easy. Members of the spiritual chivalry, defenders of Christianity on all fronts, who are simultaneously members of a Masonic Lodge (expressing relativistic, rationalistic, illuminist, and anticlerical thoughts), seem, at the very least, to be individuals with confused ideas.

Such a situation usually occurs when an individual possesses a superficial and poor understanding of the specifics of chivalry and the peculiarities of Freemasonry. A similar condition may also arise when a person experiences profound existential distress. With these premises, at the end of this introductory note, the author states that he would be pleased if even a single reader were prompted to reflect on the incongruity of dual membership and the fact that, as the Gospel teaches, one cannot serve two masters[11].

[11] Matt.: 6, 24 and Luke: 16, 13.

The Order of the Temple Today: the Order that Doesn't Exist

When referring to a chivalric association, the term 'Order' generally indicates a category with a high degree of prestige and recognition compared to the prerogatives of a simple association or brotherhood. In the Catholic Church, the term 'religious order' refers to a society of common life approved by an ecclesiastical authority whose members shape their lives according to the principles of evangelical perfection and take the perpetual vows of poverty, obedience, and chastity.

The Templar knighthood was effectively a religious order, possessing all these requirements. However, no universal or standardized definition determines, today, when a chivalric association can be considered an 'Order'. It is common for some groups, born in recent times under the legal form of an association, to self-proclaim as an 'Order'. This fact contributes to serious confusion.

Suppose we refer to the Poor fellow soldiers of Christ and the Temple of Solomon (or of Jerusalem). In that case, we must acknowledge that there are various international associations today whose members qualify as 'Templars' and, therefore, members of the Order of the Temple. For some groups, it is a symbolic, ideal, or metaphorical connection, and their members may define themselves as Neo Templars. In other cases, there is a strong assertion and conviction of being the 'true heirs', the 'true descendants' of the Order of the Temple.

This assertion immediately poses a serious historical problem since, as we know from documents, the Order was dissolved by Pope Clement V on March 22, 1312, with the famous papal bull *Vox in excelso* and never reactivated.

A - The Claim that the Order of the Temple has Continued Uninterrupted to the Present Day

The assertion that the Order of the Temple has persisted without interruption until the present day has sparked astonishment, disbelief, and subsequently, great perplexity among scholars due to historical inconsistencies and anachronisms inherent in this statement. Indeed, while the Order of the Temple was, on the one hand, a religious chivalric order under the protection of the Pope, established to defend the Holy Land and the Holy Sepulchre, on the other hand, one must question if and how the Order could have continued to operate clandestinely with values and principles completely different from its original ones after its suspension.

No documents supporting that claim have been found in the nine centuries that separate us from that historical period. There exists, to be truthful, something: documents deemed false by experts (such as the famous Charter of Jean-Marc Larmenius) that only confirm the attempt, carried out in Masonic circles in the late 18th century, to lend credence to a Templar Order operating clandestinely on a path that could be described as heretical.

While there are no difficulties in defining the orders of Malta, the Golden Fleece, and the Holy Sepulchre as 'orders', in many other cases, the term seems inappropriate. This is because chivalric orders, like those mentioned earlier, are characterized by a prestigious and documented history, a well-defined internal structure, and a certain degree of official recognition from governments or ecclesiastical institutions.

Difficulties and inconsistencies arise and become apparent when delving into the historical, spiritual, and religious evaluation of the self-proclaimed 'heirs of the Order of the Temple'.

B - Modern Templar Organizations: An Exploration of Continuity and Divergence

Several 'Templar' organizations have gained some notoriety in the past decades. Without claiming to rank them by importance, prevalence, number of followers, or historical prominence, some of these include O.S.M.T.J., S.M.O.T.J., O.T.S., O.T.J.C., S.M.T.H.O., S.O.E.T., OR.MO.TE, O.S.M.T.H., O.N.T.O., O.S.M. T.H.U.

Chronicles testify that these 'orders' have often experienced difficulties among themselves due to internal disputes, rivalries, and the personal ambitions of their 'Grand Masters.' Despite these conflicts, all the mentioned chivalric institutions share references to the Templar Knighthood, specifically the Poor Fellow-Soldiers of Christ, not only in name and declared historical connections but also in the manner of liturgical celebrations, the peculiarities of investiture rites and the attire adopted by members during official events.

In addition to these external similarities, the 'Templar orders' internal organization includes roles and hierarchies in line with medieval chivalric tradition. All these factors emphasize historical continuity with the ancient Order, regardless of its still-in-force suspension.

Nevertheless, a fundamental fact should be noted: the 'heirs' of the Templar Knighthood today profess a religious vision incompatible with Catholic Christian doctrine. They endorse esoteric and initiatory knowledge, contrary to Pauline's vision, venerate the red ouroboros, exalt Cathar thought, and practice the doctrine of salvation through knowledge (gnosis).

Delgado Galindo M., for many years Undersecretary of the Pontifical Council for the Laity, a Vatican structure with competence in the matter at hand, expressed himself as follows:

> These attempts to restore the Order of the Templars are illegitimate; however, they have generated significant confusion among the faithful. The presence of high prelates at

> these associations' liturgical celebrations and investiture ceremonies, as well as their acceptance of positions within them (Spiritual Protector, Grand Prior, etc.), undoubtedly does not contribute to clarifying this issue.

With a circular letter from the General Secretary (protocol no. 581/05/GEN) dated June 6, 2005, addressed to parish priests, rectors of churches, and chapels of the Diocese of Rome, the Vicariate of Rome took a position on the 'neo-Templar knights.' Let's see a part of it:

> Dear [clergy], reports of celebrations in churches and chapels of our Diocese related to the so-called Orders of the Templars, with so-called investitures of new knights, often reach this Vicariate. On behalf of the Cardinal Vicar, I hasten to inform you that, as repeatedly clarified by L'Osservatore Romano, the Holy See recognizes and protects only the Sovereign Military Order of Malta and the Equestrian Order of the Holy Sepulchre of Jerusalem. Therefore, Reverend parish priests, rectors of churches and public chapels, or even those of religious institutes, are invited to reject requests for the use of the same churches and chapels presented by unrecognized Orders, especially those concerning Eucharistic celebrations intended

D - Reflections on the Restoration of the Templar Order and the Relationship with the Catholic Church

Taking a stance on reconstructing and recognizing the Order of the Temple becomes challenging and antithetical to history today. The Order of the Temple is dead and buried. Spiritual chivalry (the Poor Fellow-Soldiers of Christ, as supported by Bernard de Clairvaux in its origins) is a distant reality incompatible with the goals and principles upheld by each of those 'sovereign, military, Jerusalemite' orders that can be found today on the internet.

Suppose there are chivalric groups with deep Catholic faith desiring to establish a new Templar order. In that case, they would be unwelcome not only to Freemasonry but also to the Catholic clergy. The Church of Rome, following the suspension of the Templar Order, has laid to rest anything related to the Templar chivalry and, more generally, any form of new chivalric Order.

The Holy See recognizes its official orders: the Supreme Order of Christ, the Order of the Golden Spur, the Order of Pius IX, the Order of St. Gregory the Great, and the Order of St. Sylvester. Additionally, it recognizes and protects the Sovereign Military Order of Malta (S.M.O.M.) and the Equestrian Order of the Holy Sepulchre of Jerusalem (O.E.S.S.G.).

It seems fair to say that Freemasonry operates on two levels regarding the Christian faith. At the level of peripheral lodges, Masons, during their ritual lodge meetings, open the Book of the Sacred Law (historically and traditionally the Bible) on which, however, they place the square and compass crossed. During oaths, they place their hands on the Bible, and in the case of a family member's death, it is quite common for Masons to consult a Catholic priest and organize church funerals. Many Masons, in the secrecy of their affiliation, get married in the Church.

Similarly, lodges often undertake meritorious actions (fundraising for charity, support for sick or distressed brothers, etc.) by individual knights/masons or the group. However, it should be noted that these commendable behaviours and charitable works are not considered sufficient to change the Catholic Church's view of Freemasonry and the high chivalric degrees within it.

The reasons for the existing rupture between the Church of Rome and various Masonic obediences are deep, clear, and to this day seem impossible. As revealed in the careful and reflective reading of this text, they are based on the centuries-old attempt by the high degrees of Freemasonry to destroy the Catholic Church. The ambition to seek the end of the suspension of the Templar Order from the Holy See, draining its original values, principles, and spiritual peculiarities, is also part of this destructive endeavor.

Spiritual Chivalry

Since ancient times, humanity has sought a connection with the unknown and the sacred by establishing boundaries and delineating a threshold between these two realms. To signify the transition into an unfamiliar world beyond this limit, pillars were erected as symbols of the event. An example of this is seen in the Pillars of Hercules.

In 826 BC, the construction of the Temple in Jerusalem, commissioned by King Solomon, was completed. After its destruction by Nebuchadnezzar, King of Babylon, in 586 BC, the Jewish people rebuilt the second Temple around 536 BC, following their return from the Babylonian exile. The Temple underwent various phases, including restoration by Herod the Great and subsequent destruction by Emperor Titus in 70 AD.

Similar to the Temple of Jerusalem entrance, two columns named Jachin and Boaz, representing Stability and Strength, were placed. These symbolic names, found in the Bible[13], were later adopted by Freemasonry as part of its identity.

In the early 12th century, knights from southern France, led by Hugues de Payns and supported by Bernard de Clairvaux, settled in Jerusalem. Known as *Milites Templi or Knights of the Paupera Militia Christi*, they emphasized their connection to

[13] 1Kgs.: 7, 21; 2Chr.: 3, 17

With the bull *Considerantes dudum* of 6 May 1312, Clement V took further provisions:

> Thus, those who have been legally acquitted or will be acquitted in the future will be provided with the goods of the previous Order, with whom they can live as befits their status. With those who have confessed to the above errors, we wish that the provincial councils prudently moderate justice with mercy: the situation of these men and the extent of their confessions must be duly weighed. As for the unrepentant and repeat offenders, if there are any, God forbid, justice and canonical censorship should be observed among them. As for those who, even when questioned, denied having committed the above errors, the councils shall follow justice and equity according to the canons.

At the end of a highly politicized process, which lasted five years (October 1307 - May 1312), Jacques de Molay, XXIII Grand Master in office, was condemned to the stake as a heretic. On March 18, 1314, the sentence was carried out in Paris, on a small island in the Seine, later renamed the 'Island of the Templars.' This death marked the end of the Order.

Since around the death of Jacques de Molay, Freemasonry has created a gloomy legend, according to which the grand master, shrouded from the flames, would have cursed the king of France and the Pope, screaming that both of them would die within the year,

I thought to report in full the narrative drawn up by the chronicler Godefroy de Paris, who was present at the execution. The picture that emerges testifies to the humanity of the great master and how deep and solid his faith in Christ was.

> The master, when he saw the fire ready, immediately undressed, without any fear; he stripped naked, wearing only his shirt. He never trembled, even as he was pulled and pushed. They took him to tie him to the post and he, smiling and joyful, he let himself go. They tied his hands with a rope, and he said to them: Gentlemen, at least let me join my hands and make my prayers to God; because the moment and season have come: I see here the time of my judgment and dying suits me. God knows who is wrong and who has sinned; soon misfortune will fall on those who have unjustly condemned us. God will avenge our death. Lord, said he, know that, in truth, all those who are against us will suffer because of it. In this faith I want to die: this is my faith, and I pray to turn my face towards the Virgin Mary, from whom Christ, our Lord, was born. His request was granted. And the death took him so gently that everyone was amazed.[16]

---

[16] Godefroy de Paris, (1827), *Chronique métrique de Godefroy de Paris,* Paris, Verdiére, p. 219. Author's translation.

After these tragic events, the tasks of the new chivalry did not limit themselves to the attempt to free and defend the places where they had seen the preaching of Jesus Christ. These knights were also required to maintain a code of honour and stability in the kingdoms.

In the 13th century, the Order of Chivalry was not only concerned with military events of the Holy Land. Still, it was becoming the guarantor of the morality of the knight and loyalty to the feudal lord. At the same time, the knighthood offered protection to widows and orphans and was committed to maintaining a social balance based on justice.

Llull writes the *Llibre de l'Orde de Cavalleria* [17] to reiterate, loud and clear, that, over time, with the changes in political and social conditions, chivalry will probably be assigned new tasks; chivalry, however, cannot distance itself from faith in Christ.

The Majorcan sees a parallel between the office of the priest and the knight in that while the former teaches devotion and pity, the second reminds the people that when one behaves in an inappropriate way is always to be feared[18]. The strong bond of the knight with the Catholic religion emerges when the Christian apologist states that the squire who wishes to become a knight will have to demonstrate knowledge of the fourteen articles on which the faith is based, the ten commandments and the seven sacraments of the holy Catholic Church.

---

[17] Ramon Llull, (2021), *Llibre de l'Orde de Cavalleria,* Boves, Italia, Arabafenice.
[18] *Ivi*, p.83 and p. 117.

Like any man, the knight was given free will and, by virtue of this possibility, can make choices in complete freedom. Therefore, choices regarding the lifestyle to adopt won't be able to be the result of constraints.

Among the commitments freely chosen by the knight, we include the decision to live under the guidance of the theological virtues (faith, hope and charity) and the cardinal ones (prudence, justice, fortitude and temperance). These virtues suit the knight as, in reality, they are real weapons, spiritual weapons, essential to be able to face every battle with great safety. Llull believes that not even fortune will turn its back on such a knight, an exemplary man, a model of virtue, a person with strong self-control, a true man of God.

The knight knows that society observes him and considers him an example of faith, dedication and seriousness. In the letter to Timothy, Paul expresses himself this way: «I have fought the good fight, I have finished my race, I have kept the faith[19].» we can consider this thought as the summary of the knight's life: having such a strong faith in Christ to fight evil without respite and fear of death.

The chivalry that Llull addresses is an Order devoted to the fight against the enemies of the cross but also committed to maintaining social justice: a balancing element capable of preventing society from becoming too bigoted or too liberal.

To understand the peculiarities of spiritual chivalry,

[19] 2Tim.: 4, 7.

it is believed it is necessary to start with the analysis of the military equipment supplied to the individual knights and the different meanings that they attribute to the various weapons, both offensive ones and those aimed at their protection.

The strength of the Order of the Temple, the one led by Hugues de Payns[20], as was indicated and explained in *De Laude Novae Militiae ad Milites Templi*[21], lies in the certainty of possessing one double armor: an external one in iron (the armor, the weapons) and an internal one which is faith in Christ; Bernard wanted 'his' knights to be humble and simple, with helmets without plumes, with sober shirts devoid of flourishes. The armor had to be free of silver or gold decorations so the enemies, 'seeing them armed and not adorned, feel terror and not envy[22]'.

In the mid-thirteenth century, things began to change. Because of the huge economic resources of the emerging classes, the simple, spartan-like lifestyle of the 12th century began to give way to more permissive and courtly ways of being. Chastity also became uncomfortable, so much so that, in the 14th century, people wondered whether it wasn't better for knights to marry rather than practice occasional and messy sexuality.

---

[20] Hugues de Payns (1070 about - 1136) he was the first Grand Master of the Order of the Temple.

[21] Bernardo di Chiaravalle (san), (2020), *Elogio dei cavalieri templari,* Capua, Italia, Arte-tetra Edizioni.

[22] Diego Beltrutti, (2014), *Catechismo Templare*, Roma, Italia, Bastogi Editore, p. 117.

The changes in society induced modifications in the Order of Chivalry: the knights no longer came exclusively from noble families but also from a wealthy bourgeoisie. This new kind of knight no longer lives in poverty or not lives in a monastery; on the contrary, he flaunts his wealth. The knights' homes become status symbols, and courtly life takes over from ascetic life. Due to the strong demand for investitures, Llull draws attention to the need to thoroughly vet those applying to join in the chivalry to avoid investing in inadequate subjects, boastful people and subjects of dubious morality.

The Majorcan states emphatically that the chivalry must be reformed due to the knights' difficult and inadequate training. One of the reasons for this state of affairs is the lack of specific textbooks and adequate education on the knight's duties. This situation is dangerous, as, on the one hand, it could result in the investiture of incompetent knights, and on the other, it could allow some knights to abuse the privileges granted to them.

Llull would like the preparation of the knights to resemble, in some way, that of lawyers, doctors, and religious people who can count on dedicated schools and competent teachers.

To understand why militancy in chivalry was so coveted, we must refer to Saint Isidore of Seville[23],

---

[23] Isidoro di Siviglia, (2004), *Etimologie o Origini,* a cura di A. Valastro Canale, Torino, Italia, UTET. 2 voll.

The Duties of the Knight

The tasks assigned to the medieval knight were defined by Bernard de Clairvaux, both in *De Laude Novae Militiae ad Milites Templi*[25] and in the *Rule of the Order*[26], and later by Ramon Llull in *Llibre de l'Orde de Cavalleria*[27].

Bernard provides a glimpse into the life of warriors/monks in the fourth chapter of *De Laude*. From the text, a simple and ascetic lifestyle emerges, characterized by discipline and absolute obedience to the superior, who controls and decides on rest, attire, and sustenance. Knights who have taken the three vows of poverty, obedience, and chastity keep their hair short and have a somewhat unkempt appearance. They are kind to each other and help each other in times of fatigue to fulfill Christ's law. They are never idle; one could say they have one heart and one soul. Their day is structured around training, combat, and prayer.

In their free time, they detest activities such as dice games, chess, bird hunting, and regular hunting. Furthermore, they cannot stand mimes, fortune-tellers, storytellers, theatrical performances, and obscene songs. Even though such lapses are rare, they are never

---

25 Catechismo Templare, Roma, Italia, BastogiLibri. (*wk. cit.*).

26 Bernardo di Chiaravalle (Santo), 2022, *Scritti sui Templari. La Regola dell'Ordine e il Trattato sulla Nuova Cavalleria*, Verona, Italia, Fede & Cultura.

27 *Llibre de l'Orde de Cavalleria*, Cuneo, Italia, Araba Fenice. (*wk. cited*).

left unpunished.

When the hour of battle arrives, the Knights of the Temple arm themselves internally with faith and externally with iron. They desire strong and fast horses and are not interested in flashy trappings. They are not concerned with ostentation or glory but only with victory. They have a calm and reflective character, knowing that impulsiveness and recklessness do not aid in battle. They never succumb to panic, even in the face of cruel barbarism and overwhelming odds. They have learned to trust not only in their strength but also in the will of God's armies. In battle, they are fiercer than lions, leading Bernard to question whether it is better to call them knights or monks. In reality, they are both, as they possess the gentleness of a monk and the firmness of a knight.

From this, we can observe how the knights/monks had a lifestyle completely different from that of contemporary Masonic masters. The attitudes towards war and prayer are additional factors that make Freemasonry and spiritual chivalry entirely different in goals and practices.

In the second part of *De Laude*[28], Bernard addresses the theme of the spirituality of the Knight Templar. To become one, the knight must undertake a symbolic journey from Bethlehem to Bethany. Only then will the secular knight understand what it means to be a knight

---

[28] Diego Beltrutti di San Biagio, (2019), *Il Cavaliere del Tempio. Tra San Bernardo e la Libera Muratoria*, Boves, Italia, Araba Fenice.

of the Poor Militia of Christ. In Bethany, he will grasp the meaning of living, fighting, and perhaps dying for Jesus Christ.

None of this is part of the repertoire of the Masonic master. Hence, we must acknowledge that the duties of the Knights Templar and those of the master builders of cathedrals and Gothic art are entirely different and irreconcilable.

It will take 150 years from the establishment of the Templar Order to have a new definition of the knight's duties. This evolution is mainly due to changes in Western society. The Blessed Majorcan specifies in detail the duties of the knight in the 13th century. He does so in the second section of *Llibre de l'Orde de Cavalleria*. As evident from the text, the knight's main task is to maintain and defend the holy Catholic faith. These statements leave no room for doubt. Whether Templar or non-monastic chivalry emerged in the 13th and 14th centuries, they were not interested in esotericism, Gnosticism, alchemy, or occultism. All these branches of knowledge did not align with their interests or duties.

We know that spiritual chivalry was born to liberate and defend the Holy Sepulcher and the Holy Land. With changing political and social conditions, the Order of Chivalry realized that Bernard de Clairvaux's vision, while remaining rooted in Christian spirituality, required adjustments.

It's likely that the 'acacia brothers[29]' won't agree with these statements, noting that there is extensive literature documenting the relationships between the Templar chivalry and various secret societies[30].

However, these assessments are self-referential since the cited authors base their thinking on either a 'hidden' oral tradition or 18th-century documents drafted in a Masonic context. Among these documents, the most famous is the Charter of Larménius. It is a document dated 1314, in which Jacques de Molay, before being condemned to the stake, allegedly entrusted his office to a knight named Johannes Marcus Larmenius. Alain Demurger defines the Charter as follows:

> This document is a gross fabrication done by a friend of Fabré-Palaprat, Dr. Jacques Philippe Ledru. To appear more credible, Fabré-Palaprat added a list of clandestine Grand Masters of the Temple, from Larménius to the Duke of Cossé-Brissac,

---

[29] Acacia is considered a significant symbol in Masonic tradition. In Masonic symbolism, acacia is often associated with concepts such as immortality, innocence, and rebirth. This symbol is sometimes used to represent eternal life or the immortality of the soul.

[30] Lancianise D., 2009, *I Templari, setta esoterica. Filosofia e segreti dell'Ordine del Tempio*, Roma, Italia, Atanòr. - Marischi G., 2019, *Massoneria templare e Rosacroce. Gradi cavallereschi dal XV al XXX di rito scozzese antico ed accettato*, Acireale, Italia, Tipheret. - Cipriani D., 2019, *Templari e Rosacroce. L'ordine di Oriente,* Roma, Italia, BastogiLibri.

> massacred in 1792, including Bertrand du Guesclin, constable of Charles V. The fundamental basis for all contemporary neo-Templar movements. Some falsehoods can only deceive those who want to be deceived. Starting from them, anything is possible: historical hallucinations of those seeking their roots, charitable organizations, secret sects, and apocalyptic movements. Dozens of associations worldwide now claim their affiliation with the Temple[31].

While historians study and analyze social, political, and economic events of societies and communities, especially those of the past, based on available documents judged as truthful, usually found in State Archives or other historical archives, neo-Templar groups and some writers cling to myths, legends, and stories, even very ancient ones transmitted orally. This narrative tends to mix and confuse the real with the fantastic and the imaginary. The Charter of Larménius is one such case.

In the mid-13th century, Ramon Llull, former seneschal of James II, King of Majorca, identifies the knight's tasks in the second section of his book. Among these duties, we highlight the first three, which seem particularly significant:

---

[31] Demurger A., 2011, *Cavalieri di Cristo*. In: 'MedioEvo', n. 174. URL: *https://ora-et-labora.net/templari.html*. (*Verified 15-01-2023*).

true despot, the tyrant of all humanity.

What does Freemasonry mean when it claims the right to exercise sincere doubt and honest belief? Does it imply that the Catholic creed is dishonest? Does it suggest that the conscience and thoughts of Christ's faithful are chained by an oppressive spiritual power (read the Catholic Church)? We do not want to delve into the merits of such assertions. The point is not this; what matters is that if an individual holds this view of the Catholic Church, he can certainly join Freemasonry but can no longer consider himself a Christian.

The vision of the Masonic knight is that of the Enlightenment, where religious norms have no power to guide humanity. For the Mason, only reason possesses this power; there are many religions, but none has the truth more than another. For the deists, a god exists, but it is not the god of a particular religion. This view is interesting because it helps us understand how the idea of the Great Architect of the Universe came about. Freemasonry believes that everyone has the right to build their religion, worship their god, and question any act coming from the Church of Rome based on exclusively rational thinking.

With these premises, it is clear that Masonic knights have no common ground with the spiritual chivalry that history presents as an expression of Christianity. Christians do not reject doubt since it is part of everyday life; however, they cannot have doubts about the word of Jesus Christ, his life, his death on the cross, or his resurrection. The same goes for the Good News reported by the four evangelists or the narration of the Old

Testament.

Masons are excluded from the community of believers in Jesus Christ and, therefore, from spiritual chivalry, not for expressing some doubt about liturgical aspects or the exposition of a text, which is more than permissible, but for their constant efforts against the Church of Rome with the intention of destroying it. Yes, because supporting antidogmatic thinking, esoteric knowledge, and usurping reason means chipping away at faith in Christ.

> [...] The Papacy has always exerted a decisive influence on the fate of Italy. With the arm, the voice, the pen, and the hearts of its countless bishops, friars, nuns, and faithful from all walks of life, the Papacy finds people everywhere ready for sacrifice, martyrdom, and enthusiasm. Wherever it wishes to call upon it, it has friends who die and others who strip themselves for its love. It is an immense lever of which only a few Popes have understood the full power. (And even they have only used it to a certain extent). Today, the goal is not to rebuild this temporarily weakened power for our service: *our final aim is that of Voltaire and the French Revolution, namely, the complete annihilation of Catholicism and even the Christian idea, which, if it were to remain standing upon the ruins of Rome, would be its perpetuation later on.*

Holy Sepulchre, the Holy Land, and combat Evil, the necessity emerges for individuals not merely skilled in warfare but also possessing unwavering spiritual motivation, an indispensable attribute.

Spiritual chivalry is marked by cornerstones, or as termed in the Anglo-Saxon world, landmarks. These are defining and irrevocable tenets, some rooted in history while others arise from contemporary societal shifts:

- The knight must harbour a mature, solid, unshakable faith in Christ.
- Loyalty to the Pope and Christian patriarchs is paramount, representing the highest spiritual authority through apostolic succession, ecumenism, prestige, and diffusion.
- The knight cannot align with self-referential, unrecognized Churches lacking full sacramental and canonical communion with each other and the Church of Rome.
- Membership in churches governed by bishops and/or patriarchs of dubious consecration or established through self-consecration is forbidden.
- The spiritual knight must never be subject to temporal power external to the Order itself.
- Acceptance into the Order is by a Prior[38] possessing a certain and recognized *fons honorum*.

[38] The order of chivalry is governed by a Prior or Grand Prior, as within the order, there is only one Master: Jesus Christ.

- Investiture by a 'Master' with Masonic lodges or self-proclaimed titles is prohibited.
- Acceptance into the knighthood of Christ occurs in a consecrated church.
- The investiture ceremony, preceded by a vigil of arms, transpires in the presence of a priest.
- The prospective knight swears on the Bible, publicly attesting fidelity to God and the Catholic Church.
- The unwavering objective of spiritual chivalry is the defence of the Holy Land, the Holy Sepulchre, and Christianity.
- The knight is devoted to safeguarding widows, orphans, and vulnerable individuals.
- The commitment is not to wage a 'holy' war but a 'just[39]' war, acknowledging that there is nothing 'holy' in war.
- War may only be declared by a recognized authority with legitimate grounds, as it is an extreme measure adopted when Evil persists and cannot be halted through alternative means[40].

---

[39] Saint Augustine provides two pillars of support for the 'bellum iustum' (just war): law and ethics. Consequently, for the saint, the 'just war' is unquestionably the 'war against evil,' which, however, can only be declared by an authority that, legally, has the right to do so.

[40] In this regard, Bernard de Clairvaux, in *De Laude Novae Militiae ad Milites Templi*, employs the concept of 'malecidio,' that is, the necessity to carry out an armed intervention aimed at the destruction of Evil. The saint, however, specifies that this solution

- The knight pledges not to raise the sword against another brother in Christ.

In the contemporary era, spiritual chivalry has evolved, witnessing a diminished need to engage in overseas conflicts for the defence of the Holy Sepulcher and the Holy Land. In light of this transformation, the mission of spiritual chivalry has acquired a heightened awareness of additional principles that underscore its commitment to safeguarding core Christian values. As such:

- The knighthood is dedicated to protecting life in all its phases, from its inception.
- The spiritual knight acknowledges and upholds the intrinsic structure of the family, conceived as a union between a man and a woman founded on marriage.
- The knight champions the fundamental right of parents to educate their children in the Christian tradition.
- Individuals affiliated with a 'pseudo-Order,' typically a neo-Templar association lacking a substantiated and well-documented historical tradition, are not recognized as true knights within the spiritual order.

---

can only be adopted if every other peaceful resolution of the dispute has been attempted without success.

Does a Chivalric Esotericism Really Exist?

To the question of whether there was esotericism within Christianity and then within the Templar Chivalry, something akin to Masonic esotericism, we must answer negatively, even though this topic has seen many disputes among opposing factions. Nevertheless, this belief exists especially among writers, often biased, who tend to confuse documentary historical reality with an unproven oral tradition[41].

The issue of the alleged existence of Christian esotericism starts from a passage in Matthew:

> Then the disciples came and said to him, 'Why do you speak to them in parables?' And he answered them, «To you, it has been given to know the secrets of the kingdom of heaven, but to them, it has not been given[42].»

The term 'parable' should not be frightening. The parable falls within the communicative mode chosen by Jesus to address complex subjects, themes not easily

---

[41] Cipriani D., 2017, *I cavalieri Templari. Storia, segreti, filosofia, spiritualità,* Roma, Italia, BastogiLibri. - Cipriani D., 2019, *Templari e Rosacroce. L'ordine di Oriente.* (*wk. cited*) - Masala A., *All' ombra del Tempio. Notizie, curiosità e misteri sui cavalieri templari*, Roma, Italia, Atanòr.

[42] Matthew 13:10-11, ESV.

distinguish truth from lies.

Suppose some authors have written about Templar esotericism. In that case, they have done so by referring to confessions extracted under torture from some unfortunate knight during the famous trial in Paris, which ended with the burning at the stake of Jacques de Molay and many other knights. Obviously, considering the severe torture to which the victims were subjected, we cannot take at face value what they narrated. Telling the torturers what they wanted to hear was one of the strategies employed by the victims in an attempt to save their lives.

Most books on this subject refer to a vaguely defined 'oral tradition' and/or a 'secret narrative': captivating stories based only on remote hypotheses.

This helps us understand how some writers, often active advocates of Freemasonry, have confused their particular view of history and chivalry with the desire to proclaim to the world: see? Here is the red thread that connects the builders of Solomon's Temple to the Templars and the Templars to medieval Freemasonry. These are the stories that appeal to publishers because mystery and the occult are themes that sell.

Over the centuries, around the Templar Order, legends have arisen that have gradually developed to the point of distorting or even replacing historical facts, enriching them with a fascinating aura of mystery.

As mentioned earlier, in the extensive literature on the Templar theme, we must distinguish publications from reliable, highly experienced, authoritative, and objective historians[46] regarding the subject at hand from those of scholars driven by great enthusiasm due to their evident sympathy for the Masonic institution[47].

Among the first, we want to remember the medievalist Régine Pernoud, director of the center Jeanne d'Arc d'Orléans, who dismisses as 'demented and foolish[48]' the alleged uninterrupted continuity of Templar knowledge with Masonry. Henry Coil, in his Encyclopedia of Freemasonry, addresses the issue in this way:

> Many writers have invented or repeated legends of purely fanciful characters in an attempt to link the Modern Masonic Templar Knights with the medieval Order. However, this was already extinct for over four hundred years when the first signs of the modern (Masonic) Order appeared; not a single trace dating back to 1314 that connected them to the Templar knights has ever been found[49].

---

[46] Demurger A., *Vita e morte dell'Ordine dei Templari.* (*wk. Cited*) - Demurger A., 2006, *I Templari. Un ordine cavalleresco cristiano nel Medioevo*, Milano, Italia, Garzanti.

[47] Cipriani D. *I Cavalieri Templari. (wk. cited).* - Marischi G., *Massoneria Templare e Rosacroce. Gradi cavallereschi dal XV al XXX di Rito Scozzese Antico ed Accettato. (wk. cited).* - Cipriani D., *Templari e Rosacroce. L'Ordine di Oriente.* (*wk. cited*).

[48] Pernoud R., 1993, *I Templari,* Milano, Italia, Effedieffe, p. 11.

[49] Coil H. W., 1961, *Coil's Masonic Enciclopedya*, Richmond, USA, Macoy Publishing & Masonic
Supply, p. 119.

In essence, the much-acclaimed and exalted 'Templar Mysteries,' always surrounded by an aura of secrecy, the occult, and enigma, are not a historical reality unless one wants to subvert all the rules that have been used since time immemorial to define a fact as historical. Some of these narratives make us smile and would probably be very successful if used for the set of a commemorative film.

Drawing on my memory, I mention some: in an attempt to recover elements of the tradition considered lost, the Knights Templar would have secretly collaborated with Gnostic initiatory sects, even with the Assassins sect, that of the Old Man of the Mountain[50]. According to this narrative style, even the Templar flag, the *Beauceant*, would have been made with that particular design to express the Gnostic concept of cosmic dualism, that is, the struggle between Good and Evil.

Staying within a 'traditional' view, and therefore closely related to Freemasonry, other writers tell us that the Templars would have had a continuity of thought with the Celts and that Bernard de Clairvaux himself possessed initiative and Gnostic knowledge.

Entering a bookstore reveals the availability of a myriad of publications with titles such as 'The Mystery of the Holy Grail,' 'The Priory of Sion,' 'The Lost Treasure of the Templars,' 'The True Code of the

---

[50] Ḥasan-i Ṣabb (abot 1034 - 1124) is a Persian religious leader, the head of the Nizari Ismailis, a group also known as 'the sect of the Assassins.'

Templars,' 'The Worshippers of Baphomet,' 'The Secret Rites of the Templars,' and so on.

This approach to telling history, with great sensationalism, little objectivity, and without having certain sources, helps us understand how the Masonic narrative of Templarism relies exclusively on unverified and unverifiable events, on legendary, mythical, and fairy-tale foundations.

Some writers, probably caught up in imaginative speculations and trapped in a Gnostic view of reality, have gone so far as to hypothesize that Jesus was not the Son of God but only an 'enlightened' man. For others, Jesus would have been a Rabbi, part of the Essene community of Wadi Qumran. It is curious to note that Masonic literature has given great credence to apocryphal and Gnostic Gospels to the detriment of the canonical ones.

The way of narrating history *ad usum delphini* is undoubtedly the result of the presence in the market of a certain type of reader, uncritical readers who devour any sensational truth. These individuals are intrigued, fascinated, and captivated by what is narrated in many Masonic texts, ranging from Kabbalah to Hermeticism, from Gnosticism to magic, from alchemy to theosophy, from occultism to Rosicrucianism, from Cagliostro (G. Balsamo) to Louis Claude de Saint-Martin, from Annie Besant to Helena Blavatsky, just to name a few.

While the Church of Rome asserts the non-existence of Christian esotericism, as evidenced by the findings of the early ecumenical councils, the opposite occurs with

Freemasonry. This institution advocates knowledge accessible only to a select circle of initiates, a knowledge that cannot and should not be disclosed. This secret, esoteric knowledge, internal to the various degrees and rituals of Freemasonry, is intriguing. What piques interest is not just learning that Freemasonry considers itself the heir of Templar chivalry but also that it claims inheritance from many other esoteric experiences. The Rosicrucian Order is one such example.

In 1610, a booklet with the curious title *The Chemical Wedding of Christian Rosenkreutz in the Year 1459* appeared in Strasbourg. In addition to dealing with the esoteric, initiatic journey toward the illumination of Christian Rosenkreutz, the text seeks to unveil, through magic, the mysteries of nature and its occult aspects. The Rosicrucian order, since its appearance, has proven to be a mysterious, secretive structure characterized by a complex mystical, gnostic, and kabbalistic vision. Rosicrucian and Gnostic thought converge in the 18th degree of the R.·.S.·.A.·.A.·., the degree of *the Sovereign Prince Rosicrucian.* Albert Pike summarized Rosicrucian thought: «Man is God, the son of God, and there is no other God than Man[51]».

It is natural that the Catholic Church, from then on, has harboured resentment toward this organization, as it stands in clear opposition to the main Christian tenets. It is not our task to analyze all the writings published

[51] Pike A., (2010), *Morals, Dogma and Clausen's Commentaries*, Foggia, Italia, Bastogi, p. 172.

toward the end of the 17th century with clear anti-Catholic intentions.

We will only mention, for example, the text *Lux in Tenebris*[52] by Comenius (Jan Amos Kominsky). In this work with prophetic undertones, the destruction of the Church of Rome and the death of the pope, René Guénon reminds us that during the Congress of Free Thinkers held in Brussels in 1880, Annie Besant concluded her speech by stating that the purpose of the Theosophical Society was to: «fight against Rome and its priests, to struggle everywhere against Christianity, and to drive God out of the Heavens[53]».

According to the French esotericist, the goal of Helena Petrovna Blavatsky and Annie Besant, who led the Theosophical Society for years, was not to restore Eastern esotericism[54]. In fact, according to the two theosophists, they expressed, «Our goal is not to restore Hinduism but to erase Christianity from the face of the Earth[55].»

Another esoteric strand within Freemasonry is associated with the anthroposophical movement[56] of

---

[52] *Lux in tenebris Hoc est Prophetiae Donum.* URL: *https://www.digitale-sammlungen.de/en/view/bsb10908652?page=,1.* (*Verified 11/11/2022).*

[53] Guénon R., (1987), *Il Teosofismo*, Carmagnola, Italia, Edizioni Arktos, vol. I, pag. 13.

[54] Guénon R., (1954), *El Teosofismo: historia de una pseudorreligión*, Buenos Aires, Argentina, Haz, p. 8.

[55] Ivi, p.9

[56] Steiner R., (2010), *Il cristianesimo esoterico e la guida spirituale dell'umanità*, Milano, Italia, Editrice Antroposofica.

Rudolf Steiner. In the early 20th century, the Slovenian pedagogue and esotericist proposed a new vision of reality, a path of knowledge capable of reconnecting human spirituality to universal spirituality. He was eager to renew Christianity in the light of Eastern philosophies, especially the esoteric vision of Buddhist thought, as he believed that the Catholic Church had betrayed its mandate and only the intervention of the Anthroposophical Society could prevent its dissolution. In this case, as well, the anthroposophical vision was in clear contrast with the statements of the Catholic Church.

The most followed esoteric path within Freemasonry is associated with the theories of René Guénon[57], the 'witness of tradition,' the scholar who emphasized the initial esoteric value of Christianity. According to the French intellectual, the Council of Nicaea (325 AD) marked the end of esoteric Christianity and the beginning of dogmatic Christianity. In that Council, the decision was made to encapsulate the esoteric truths that, according to the author, were present in early Christianity.

They would have been obscured and enclosed within the dogmatic concept of 'mystery' to protect them. Since then, according to Guénon, these truths have become unattainable and inaccessible to the human mind.

The Masonic world is a staunch and convinced supporter of the existence of an esoteric and

---

[57] Guénon R., (1977), *Il re del mondo*, Roma, Italia, Adelphi.

interpretative form of Christianity[58]. According to this viewpoint, in the Christianity of its origins, there was present an initiatic knowledge that was available only to a limited and selected group of individuals.

On this topic, we cannot omit to mention that the Magisterium of the Doctrine and Faith of the Catholic Church has pronounced itself clearly and unequivocally. It has decreed that there is only one Christianity, unitary, well-defined, 'dogmatic,' and accessible to all those who wish to understand it. With the term 'dogmatic,' the Church of Rome asserts that there is only one correct interpretation of the thought of Jesus Christ, the official one. While these words reassure the Christian, this way of experiencing Christianity in dogmatic terms is a source of serious concern for those who see it as an attack on freedoms, particularly freedom of thought and interpretation, beyond the closure to any form of dissent.

A Masonic brother, active at the Giordano Bruno Lodge No. 852 in the East of Ferrara (Italy), 'carved a table' (May 13, 2011) titled *Compatibility between the Catholic Church and Freemasonry*. Let's see an excerpt:

> In one of his presentations in September 1971, Brother Giovanni Pica, then Sovereign Grand Commander of the Ancient and

---

[58] Besant A., (2011), *Il Cristianesimo esoterico,* Vicenza, Italia, Edizioni Teosofiche Italiane

> Accepted Scottish Rite[59], wrote: the idea of a personal God, rewarding or punishing, was necessary for people of the past who, without it, would not have known how to impose moral rules conducive to the development of their spirit and the society in which they lived. However, the dominant factor in human history is 'the constant progress of intelligence, the successive conception of truths of every order,' so the modern, evolved man can no longer be satisfied with an outdated idea that is no longer necessary for his further development but rather hinders his evolution precisely because it is outdated. The universal character of every religion 'is to respond to the intellectual state of the time. Every religion replaces a more primitive cult, and it is replaced in turn'; this is why Freemasonry, in its perpetual anxiety for progress, distinguishes itself from religions, which it considers relics of the past, venerable yes, but still obstacles today to the free development of the human spirit.

We believe that these statements, coming from an authoritative figure such as the Sovereign Grand Commander of the Ancient and Accepted Scottish Rite, describe the true feelings of Freemasons towards

---

[59] *Compatibilità tra Chiesa cattolica e Massoneria*, Loggia Giordano Bruno all'Oriente di Ferrara, Italia. URL: *https://www.loggiagiordanobruno.com/20110513-compatibilita-fra-chiesa-cattolica-e-massoneria. html (Verified 06/11/2022).*

religion, especially the Catholic one. Religion would be an outdated idea, no longer necessary, a true 'relic of the past.'

On the other hand, it is believed that the dogmatic vision, which so much unsettles the Masons, seeks, above all, to preserve the purity of the original message of Jesus Christ, preventing anyone from removing, adding, or modifying the words of the Master and his successors on the throne of Peter.

In essence, the dogmatism present in the Catholic Church should be understood as follows: there is only one interpretation, the official one that comes from the Holy See; any other reading, any other hypothesis is unacceptable. Every individual, including Masons, is free to see evil where they believe it exists: in any action, in any institution, and therefore also in the Catholic Church and its documents. However, the act of sharing, discussing, reconciling, and then standardizing the guidelines of worship, the ways of 'being Christians' on a global level, seems to be an extremely positive operation.

Let's not forget that the Middle Ages saw the birth of many mystics in the lands overlooking the Mediterranean, the cradle of Christianity. Some of them became saints of the Catholic Church, while others gradually distanced themselves so much from the official doctrine that they were considered heretics. The teachings of these groups were banned because they could not be accepted, being discordant and sometimes openly conflicting with the official creed of the Catholic

Church.

This happened to the Fraticelli and the Patari, the Bogomils and the Cathars, the Albigenses, the Waldenses, and the Dolcinians, just to name a few. All these religious groups, despite having different spiritual experiences, are united by the fact that they possess a secret doctrine. This esoteric vision was unacceptable for Christianity, both in the past and today.

Shedding Some Light on Freemasonry

The Grand Orient of Italy (G.·.O.·.I.·.) is the oldest Masonic obedience in Italy, having been ritually established in Milan on June 20, 1805. It defines itself as follows: 'A universal initiatic order of a traditional and symbolic nature aimed at the perfection and elevation of Man and the Human Family[60].'

As for the word freemason, it derives from maçon, a term in the French language that means 'mason'; the term 'mason' is used in the English language. Usually, the term is preceded by franc in French and free in English to emphasize the condition of a free mason.

Members of Freemasonry like to think and assert that the roots of their institution are lost in the mists of time. However, with these foundations, it is not easy for historians to establish a definite date for the beginning of Freemasonry. There are indeed irrefutable documents, but they are available only from the early 18th century; if one wishes to refer to earlier periods, we can only say that there is a lack of documentation.

Freemasonry, also known as Free Masonry, is an initiatic society, as the 'profane,' the 'non-Mason,' must undergo an initiation ritual to become a part of it. By

---

[60] G.·.O.·.I.·., *Principi, Finalità e Metodi*. URL: *https://www.grandeoriente.it/chi-siamo/identita-del-grande-oriente-d-italia/principi-finalita-metodi/* (*Verified 26/06/2022*).

established practice, profanes must be tiled[61]; in other words, they can be accepted into the institution by co-optation only after careful and thorough individual evaluation. Regarding principles and purposes, the Grand Orient of Italy states:

> Embracing the Ancient Charges, it pursues the quest for truth and the perfection of Man and the Human Family; it works to extend to all men the bonds of love that unite the Brothers; it advocates tolerance, self-respect, and respect for others, freedom of conscience, and thought. It renders due obedience and scrupulously observes the Constitutional Charter of the Italian democratic state and the laws inspired by it[62].

Once entered into the Masonic institution, a well-structured path of cultural growth opens up to the neophyte, typically lasting at least three years. This period will serve the neophyte to progress through the first three degrees: from apprentice to Fellow Craft and then to master. These transitions are connected and dependent on progress in historical, philosophical, and esoteric studies and the presentation of one's advancement in Masonic art before the lodge brothers. Upon reaching the degree of master, if desired, the adept

[61] With this term, Freemasons refer to the interviews that must be conducted with aspiring candidates.
[62] G.·.O.·.I.·., *Principi, Finalità e Metodi*. (*wk. cited)*.

can continue their studies within the rites[63].

Although Freemasonry proclaims its universality and the spread of brotherhood throughout the earth, there is no single 'obedience,' meaning a single chain of command. It may seem strange, but today, in the world, there are no fewer than 418 specific Masonic groupings. These obediences are sometimes in conflict with each other (i.e., they do not mutually recognize each other), although, in the majority of cases, they do recognize and cooperate.

What are the reasons for such fragmentation? Prioritizing human nature would not be a mistake. Struggles, accusations, and disputes are often the result of personal rivalries and enmities between individuals unwilling to cede power to others. Another reason can be found in the relationships that various obediences maintain with the Catholic Church; the presence of different perspectives, particularly varying degrees of anticlericalism, has given rise to divisions, leading to actual schisms within the Orients[64].

These mentioned are nothing more than examples; given the numerous reasons for the establishment of so many obediences, it is not possible to list them exhaustively. While there are groups (such as the G.:.O.:.I.:.) practicing a more traditional Freemasonry, which involves the membership of males only, there are

---

63 The Rites are specific cultural paths of in-depth study that Freemasonry offers to Master Masons.

64 With this term, we refer to a place where a Masonic lodge is located and operates.

others more innovative that allow the initiation of women as well. In more recent times, obediences consisting exclusively of women[65] have been established. As mentioned above, some 'Orients' are more anticlerical than others. Some obediences could be considered extremely private, if not secret, while others are more open. For a variety of reasons: social, religious, linguistic, political, ethnic, etc., it is not easy to provide a definition that can describe and encompass all obediences and Masonic realities.

> The G∴O∴I∴ works for the Glory of the Great Architect of the Universe; observes the Ancient Duties, customs, and traditions of the Order; adopts rituals in line with Masonic Tradition; opens the book of the Sacred Law on the Altar of the Temple and places the Square and Compasses upon it; follows symbolism in teaching and esotericism in the Royal Art; applies the Masonic distinction in the three Degrees of Apprentice, Fellow Craft, and Master; teaches the legend of the Third Degree; refrains from discussing matters of politics and religion; initiates only men who are free and of good character, without distinction of origin, citizenship, social status, political, or religious opinions; is inspired by the Trinomial Freedom, Equality, and Brotherhood [66].

---

[65] In 1990, the Grand Lodge of Female Masonry of Italy (GLMFI) was established.

[66] G∴O∴I∴, *Principi, Finalità e Metodi.* (*wk. cited*).

The institution is quite restrictive and rigid in admitting new members, aware that not all individuals may feel drawn or be capable of following an initiatic path. Freemasonry is not interested in a massive increase in its membership numbers. What matters for the institution is to work for the future and identify individuals worthy of being guided along an initiatic path. These individuals will be assisted in approaching esoteric studies and working on themselves.

Freemasonry, contributing to the perfection of each brother, aims to: «Build Temples to Virtue, dig dark and deep prisons for Vice, and work for the Good and progress of humanity[67]».

Documents tell us that Freemasonry was officially established in Great Britain at the beginning of the 18th century, precisely on June 24, 1717. On the day of St. John, in London, at the inn 'Goose and Gridiron,' four lodges gathered. The purpose was to organize and centralize the activities of lodges in the London area. In a few years, with the participation of many other lodges, the 'Grand Lodge of England' was formed.

If instead, we rely on oral tradition, Freemasonry traces its origin to the years of the construction of Solomon's Temple[68]. It places great emphasis on the figure of the director of works, Hiram Abiff (or

---

[67] Farina S., *Il libro completo dei rituali massonici*. (*wk. cited*). p. 68.
[68] Construction began in 967 B.C. and ended in 960 B.C. The Babylonian king Nebuchadnezzar II destroyed it 410 years later.

Chiram). While the Bible[69] qualifies this character as the king of Tyre[70], in Freemasonry, he is the chief architect overseeing the construction of the Temple.

The Masonic legend, still practiced today in the third degree, recounts the story of the assassination of Hiram. This episode reminds us how three envious companions, namely Jabal, Jubal, and Tubalcain, murdered Master Hiram during a lunch break. This occurred because Hiram refused to hand over the 'password of the Master,' a kind of pass that would have allowed them to be admitted to the third degree of master. Mortally wounded, Hiram fell to the floor of the Temple, saying, «Rather a death than violate the secret entrusted to me[71]».

It is not clear what event or spark gave birth to speculative Freemasonry. We know that Freemasonry, originating from medieval guilds and corporations of masons, sculptors, and carpenters active during the construction of Gothic cathedrals, was initially termed 'operative Freemasonry.' This is because its members were individuals who worked manually in various construction sectors.

---

[69] The character is mentioned 22 times in the Bible, specifically in: 2 Samuel; 1 Kings; 1 Chronicles; 2 Chronicles.

[70] It should be remembered that in addition to Hiram, king of Tyre, the Bible also mentions "the son of a widow of the tribe of Naphtali; his father was from Tyre. He worked in bronze, was full of wisdom, understanding, and skill to do any work in bronze. He went to King Solomon and carried out all the work he ordered. (1 Kings 7:14).

[71] Farina S., *Il libro completo dei rituali massonici*. (*wk. cited*). p. 68.

At some point, the masons decided to open the doors to the lodges, allowing not only the professionals of the masonic arts but also individuals unrelated to that trade, such as apothecaries, doctors, lawyers, etc., to become members.

With the establishment of lodges where the number of profanes (individuals not working manually in the construction field) outweighed the master masons, the decline of operative Freemasonry began. Thus, 'speculative Freemasonry' was born. Through its initiatory rituals, it sought to connect to a secret tradition that, according to its followers, had been passed down orally since the construction of Solomon's Temple.

This legendary, mythical transfer of secret knowledge represents the wisdom of Freemasonry as a 'traditional initiatory society.' As the number of 'speculative' Freemasons and intellectuals grew, elements such as Kabbalah, occultism, alchemy, and hermetic texts entered the lodges. In 1738, the Grand Lodge of London approved new Constitutions, banning discussions on politics and religion within the lodges and reaffirming the concept of the Grand Architect of the Universe as the Supreme Being. Gradually, a process of de-Christianization of rituals began.

Another outcome in this regard was achieved with the 1815 Constitutions, which removed any privileges associated with the Catholic religion, considering it as the religion traditionally practiced in the country. These constitutions also established that there were no differences between religions.

In France, Freemasonry emerged around 1725. Its members were predominantly nobles, wealthy bourgeoisie, and even Gallican clergy, i.e., those opposed to the supremacy of the Bishop of Rome. Masonic lodges soon became crucibles of secular and Enlightenment thought.

The Masonic institution aims to guide its members to the stage of inner enlightenment, restoring order and unity in the human being after harmonizing it with 'the universal laws that inform the world, which are reproduced in symbols and, by the hermetic motto *as above, so below*, are also intuited by man[72].'

Although the Constitutions of Anderson in 1723, the Landmarks, and the Declaration of Principles[73] confirm an absolute belief in a Supreme Being referred to as G.:.A.:.D.:.U.:. (Grand Architect of the Universe), these documents do not refer to the God of Christians. Freemasonry overlooks what is fundamental and non-negotiable for a Christian, namely the figure of Jesus Christ, the Holy Spirit, the Holy Trinity, resurrection, forgiveness of sins, and eternal life.

In their journey of growth within the lodge, the modern mason must undergo a symbolic ritual of death, followed by a ceremony of rebirth as a 'new man.' Suppose the mason's ideal, expressed in operative

---

[72] Gianluca Paolucci, (2012), *Esperienza e Ritualità Massoniche nella letteratura della 'Goethezeit'*. Dottorato di ricerca in culture e letterature comparate, Roma, Università Roma Tre, p. 45.

[73] *Dichiarazione dei Princìpi approvata dal Convento dei Supremi Consigli Confederati riuniti a Losanna nel settembre 1875*. (*wk. cited*). p. 148.

terms, is to construct a real building, a church, a temple, in speculative terms. In that case, the mason's ideal is to build the 'inner temple,' realizing their individuality while contributing to the creation of an 'external temple' (i.e., a better, more humane, rational, and just society).

Thus, the Masonic institution becomes an educator, shaping 'new men.' In the lodge, the adept is instructed to become, when ready, eligible to receive a series of ritual passages or, as the members say, an 'increase in light.' With the growth of inner enlightenment, the neophyte can advance to the degree of Apprentice, then to Fellow Craft, and finally to Master. Freemasonry is also defined as an initiatory society precisely because of its method, where specific rites of passage characterize entry and various degree advancements.

Freemasonry declares to operate «for the good and progress of the Homeland and Humanity[74]» and defines itself as universal since the principles it defends and the goals it aims to achieve are identical and valid worldwide. Its mission does not end within the lodges, as the institution asks its members to act externally, in the profane world, to contribute to the construction of a new society free from dogmas and prejudices.

With the opening of lodges to the bourgeoisie, professionals, public servants, intellectuals, military personnel, and artists began to meet and work together. Various motivations led these individuals to join the

---

[74] Farina Salvatore, *Il libro completo dei rituali massonici*. (*wk. cied*). p. 68.

lodges despite having different social backgrounds. For some, the attraction stemmed from the mystique, secrecy, and power that have always surrounded the institution. Others were driven by simple curiosity, while some felt honoured that Freemasonry had noticed them and invited them to enter, deeming them worthy of such an honour. Another pull factor was philanthropy, the spirit of tolerance, and the prohibition of discussing politics and/or religion.

The trinity of liberty, equality, and fraternity exerted a strong attraction. This motto, present during the time of the French Revolution, has been attributed by René Guénon to Freemasonry. According to the famous French esotericist, it would not only be a motto but even an initiatic formula. In reality, upon closer inspection, the values expressed by the aforementioned trinity are also found in Christianity.

Freemasonry still demands the utmost secrecy from its members regarding the work performed, rituals, oaths, and any topic discussed within the lodge. Recently, at least in Italy, Freemasonry has replaced the term 'secrecy' with 'confidentiality' to avoid falling under the strict provisions of Law No. 177 of January 25, 1982[75].

Since its inception, Freemasonry has positioned itself against the Catholic religion and the Pope,

---

[75] The law of January 25, 1982, No. 17 - Rules for implementing Article 18 of the Constitution concerning secret associations and the dissolution of the association called "Loggia P2." In Italy this law is also known as the Tina Anselmi Law.

adopting Enlightenment ideas, advocating for the rigorous use of reason, placing great trust in the sciences, empirical methods, and progress, and promoting a secular culture and society. Catholic doctrine, traditions, and Christian values, which were previously well-accepted in society, were now labelled as 'things of the past.'

The French Masonry was the most uncompromising against religion. It is noteworthy that the Grand Orient of France even replaced the figure of the Grand Architect of the Universe with the Goddess Reason and allowed agnostic and atheist individuals to enter the lodges, thus violating one of the fundamental principles of speculative Freemasonry.

The concerns of the Holy See regarding Freemasonry have been significant from the beginning. They are entirely understandable, especially when analyzing what Freemasonry, through its prominent figures, claimed to want to implement regarding the papacy and the religion of Christ. Consider Albert Pike, a member of the Supreme Council of the Ancient and Accepted Scottish Rite, who, in the second half of the 19th century, argued that Freemasonry had an ancient Hebrew origin:

According to the author, all true dogmatic religions originate from the Kabbalah and return to it. All that is great and scientific in the religious ideals of all the Illuminati, Jacob Böhme, Emanuel Swedenborg, Saint Martin, and others comes from the Kabbalah; all Masonic associations owe their secrets and symbols to it[76].

In the context of Masonry and Secret Societies, the author quotes Elio Toaff, the Chief Rabbi of Rome, from the French edition of Elia Benamozegh's book Israel et l'Humanité[77].

> Masonic theology exists in the sense that Freemasonry has a secret and religious doctrine introduced by Rosicrucian Gnostics at the time of the merger with the Free Masons in 1717. This secret doctrine or gnosis is the exclusive prerogative of High-Degree Freemasonry or Philosophical Freemasonry[78].

The statements of Kabbalists, esotericists, rabbis, scholars of occult sciences could be taken up; texts, magazines, essays could be cited to shed light, at least on the main secret societies that, in addition to Freemasonry, operate with anticatholic purposes: the Strict Observance, the Golden Dawn, the Societas Rosicruciana in Anglia (SRIA), the Theosophical Society, the Martinists, etc. However, this would go beyond the scope of this essay. Nevertheless, we cannot help but notice a parallel between what is happening in

---

[76] Pike A., (1927), *Morals and Dogma of the Ancient and Accepted Scottish Rite of Freemasonry*, Jenkins, USA, Richmond, p. 745.
[77] Benamozegh E., (1961), *Israël et l'humanité,* Paris, France, Albin Michel.
[78] Epiphanius, (2021), *Massoneria e Sette segrete*, Napoli, Italia, Controcorrente, p.195.

European political circles and what some would like to happen in the religious field.

The spirit of the EU is to create a more homogeneous set of countries, even better if equipped with the same laws, the same economy, the same currency, the same army... so why not aspire to a single religion? Why not? However, what organization could manage such an extensive project? Freemasonry, in its High Degrees, if supported by high Jewish finance, would have the capabilities. A new religion based on ethical equivalence, Gnosticism, and relativism would no longer be Christian but a mixture of Christianity, Islam, Hinduism, Buddhism, etc., and even animistic, pagan, satanic religions. Political correctness dictates that no one should be excluded, so all philosophical systems and different religious doctrines have the right to be part of an ecumenical, fluid, shared religion. In this regard, there is already the New Age that meets these requirements.

The New Age or the Age of Aquarius, indeed, mixes and incorporates all these aspects, like in a great sabbat: matter and spirit, science and religion, animism and Christianity, God and man. However, there is a problem, an obstacle: true Catholics know that Jesus is the only begotten Son of God, and on this point, they are not conciliatory; he and no other is the way, the truth, and the life[79]. That's why there is so much animosity against the Holy See; because it, over two millennia, has

[79] 'Jesus said to him, «I am the way, and the truth, and the life. No one comes to the Father except through me».' (John 14:6, ESV)

managed to survive countless attempts at destruction.

We know, however, that dark forces do not give up. On June 25, 1995, Presbyterian Bishop William E. Swing, during a syncretistic ceremony held in the Cathedral of San Francisco, announced the establishment of the United Religions, following the Masonic thought. The ceremony was repeated in Dallas, Texas. Besides Christians, Jews, Muslims, Buddhists, Hindus, members of Wicca (neopagan movement), followers of Scientology, shamanic movements, and representatives of witchcraft were invited to join this union.

Not dissimilar to the vision of the EU is that of the UN. The United Nations today speaks of the need for Global Governance.

> The time is now ripe, indeed overdue, to build a global forum that can provide leadership in economic, social, and environmental fields[80].

In June 2000, Bishop Swing founded the United Religions Initiative (URI), an organization with a clear Theosophical influence. URI immediately received funding from George Soros, as well as from members of the Bilderberg Club and the Trilateral Commission,

---

[80] 'Our Global Neighborhood,' 1995, Report of the Commission on Global Governance, Chapter Seven - A Call to Action, Oxford, England, Oxford University Press. 'The time is now ripe - indeed overdue - to build a global forum that can provide leadership in economic, social, and environmental fields.' (Translation by the Author).

including Richard Blum and Dee Hock. Among the organization's goals was the understanding that, in an increasingly interconnected world, fundamentalist religious systems could not be accepted.

According to URI, there is a need to establish a global spiritual authority that can be accepted by everyone, regardless of geographical location. The Great Architect of the Universe is deemed fit for this task to bring order out of chaos (*Ordo ab Chao*[81]). Just as markets, economy, and communication are global in today's world, there is also a perceived need to work towards a 'global soul' on the religious plane. In essence, Christianity is no longer considered suitable.

> Militants of the so-called left work to destroy the family, culture, heritage, order, and the military; in short, the foundational structure of a traditional society, in the name of egalitarian and pacifist liberal secularism. On the other hand, those from the so-called right are engaged in dismantling small industries, craftsmanship, small agricultural businesses, and local commerce in the pursuit of wealth growth in society, free trade, and economic liberalism. Meanwhile, those in the center strive to eradicate, in the heart of the people, the idea and meaning of the word 'homeland,' all in the name of humanity and friendship among all peoples. This is accompanied by

[81] *Ordo ab Chao* is the motto that appears on the emblem of the Ancient and Accepted Scottish Rite.

> relentless advertising promoting racial mixing (strongly supported by more or less aware clergy) to uproot any remaining attachment to the true religion, the traditions that have flourished around it, and the cultural and historical roots of a people[82].

We understand, therefore, that the resistance the Catholic Church must now put into action to maintain its creed unaltered is much more severe than in the past. It has to withstand the globalist, relativist impact coming from the Bilderberg Club, the Trilateral Commission, the Group of Thirty, the Aspen Institute for Humanistic Studies, the One World Church, the Lucis Trust, the Club of Rome, the B'nai B'rith, the Pilgrim Society, Skull and Bones, and others.

All these groups are financially robust and politically influential. Nor should the attacks on the Catholic Church from within by 'progressive' prelates be underestimated.

[82] Epiphanius, *Massoneria e sette segrete. (wk. cited)*. p. 929-930.

The Thought of the Catholic Church on Freemasonry

Canon 2335 of the 1917 Code of Canon Law declared that those who joined Freemasonry (referred to here as the 'Masonic sect') or other similar associations conspiring against the Church or legitimate civil authorities would incur *ipso facto* excommunication reserved to the Apostolic See[83]. The term 'Masonic sect' is taken from Article 247 of the Synodal Constitutions of the First Roman Synod in 1960, established by Pope John XXIII.

In the last four centuries, nine popes have condemned Freemasonry, both the regular, legitimate, recognized form and the irregular ones[84], in a total of 586 documents. Despite all this, we cannot certainly assert that the problem has been resolved. Practicing and observant Catholics who, at the same time, are members of Freemasonry do not seem to have been disturbed to

---

[83] *Vi spiego perché Massoneria e Chiesa sono incompatibili*, June 1 2022, La Nuova Bussola, Nico Spuntoni intervista Padre Zbigniew Suchecki, professore alla Pontificia Facoltà di S. Bonaventura -Seraphicum. URL*: https://lanuovabq.it/it/vi-spiego-perche-massoneria-e-chiesa-sono-incompatibili* (Verified 22/08/22).

[84] A masonic obedience is considered regular when it adheres to fundamental principles, constitutions, and landmarks. Through this filter, an obedience assesses others and consequently categorizes them as regular or irregular.

learn about their excommunication.

Excommunication today has lost the legacy of being a powerful instrument it had in the Middle Ages. The Church seems to have understood that it would be better to limit excommunication, an important tool in criminal law, to serious offences by the clergy. Today, excommunications, such as those for Masons, are defined as *latae sententiae*; they are automatic excommunications, meaning that they don't need to be explicitly pronounced by an ecclesiastical authority against a specific individual.

The view of the Church on Freemasonry (*De secta Francomurariorum*) has not changed since Pope Clement XII issued the apostolic letter *In Eminenti Apostolatus Specula* on April 28, 1738. It should be noted that the judgment of Freemasonry on the Church has also not changed. Freemasonry continues to consider, as a central and non-negotiable point of its creed, that truth cannot be known and that in the journey of man towards the eternal, there are equally possible and valid truths.

> Freemasons deny the possibility of an objective knowledge of truth. [...] *The relativity of every truth* represents the basis of Freemasonry. Since the Mason rejects any faith in dogmas, he does not admit any dogma even in his lodge. [...] *Such a concept of truth is not compatible with the Catholic concept of truth, neither from the perspective of natural*

theology nor from that of the theology of revelation[85].

Another divisive theme is related to the Supreme Being. In Masonic rituals, a central place is occupied by the figure of the Grand Architect of the Universe; the situation regarding the Supreme Being could have been even worse if, instead of adopting a syncretic system of spiritual brotherhood capable of including every existing religion on the face of the earth, Freemasonry had placed nothing at the center of its spirituality.

It is evident that, for the Roman Church, it was not possible to accept this deistic conception, which took on a rather polemical tone in the 18th century. The traditional Catholic idea, based on revelation and mysteries, was opposed to reason and freedom of conscience.

The G.·.A.·.D.·.U.·.[86] and the God of Catholics are two very distant, completely different, and irreconcilable things. The Great Architect of the Universe is an immanent, obscure entity that does not reveal itself. Man does not receive solace, comfort, or support from this god. Consequently, moral behaviour depends solely on the individual's effort to be just, honest, and upright. It is understood, therefore, why the

---

[85] Declaration of the German Bishops' Conference regarding the affiliation of Catholics with Freemasonry, p. 193.

[86] The acronym G.·.A.·.D.·.U.·.. stands for 'Grande Architetto Dell'Universo' in Italian, which translates to "Great Architect of the Universe" in English.

spiritual chivalry, the heir of the *Paupera Militia Christi* and *the Orde de Cavalleria*, must be composed solely of knights with deep Christian faith.

For all contemporary spiritual knights, there is no alternative. Other solutions are not possible. One must accept and make one's own the positions of irreconcilability expressed and reiterated since Pope Clement XII.

After two hundred eighty-five years, ignorance is no longer acceptable. In various chivalric groups, expressions of the higher degrees of Freemasonry, as well as in lodges, it is not possible to continue repeating the same 'non-truths' to younger brothers. It is not possible to continue to assert that excommunications have been abolished and that today, there is no obstacle to Masons participating in religious functions and receiving the Eucharist.

Freemasonry is not interested in any particular religion since its purpose is to bring together men of all religions, regardless of various denominations. It follows that it is almost impossible for Freemasonry to identify moral principles, let alone teach them. Freemasonry is an institution founded on deism and the reasonable and reasoned existence of a Supreme Being; however, it denies the existence of a God understood as the Absolute Being revealed, good, just, and loving, and therefore cannot consider the Catholic religion. It is evident that for Freemasonry, having a morality that fulfills the requirements of Christianity or other religions is literally impossible[87].

Albert Clarin de la Rive, in his text *La Femme et l'Enfant dans la Franc-Maconnerie Universelle*, quotes (p. 588) a passage from a speech given by Albert Pike in 1889 before the high degrees of French Freemasonry. Albert Pike, a Confederate general, lawyer, and Sovereign Grand Commander of the Southern Jurisdiction of the Ancient and Accepted Scottish Rite, is considered the father of modern Freemasonry. His text, *Morals and Dogma of the Ancient and Accepted Scottish Rite of Freemasonry*, is still widely read on both sides of the ocean. Here is what de La Rive writes:

> To the crowd, I must say: we worship a God, but it is the God worshiped without superstition. To you, Sovereign Grand Inspectors General, we say this so that you may repeat it to the brothers of the 32nd, 31st, and 30th degrees: all of us initiates of the high degrees should maintain the Masonic religion in the purity of Luciferian doctrine. If Lucifer were not God, Adonai, the God of Christians, whose deeds prove his cruelty, perfidy, and hatred for man, his barbarism, and repulsion for science, would have calumniated him with his priests?
>
> Yes, Lucifer is God, and unfortunately,

[87] Card. Caro y Rodriguez J. M., 2020, *La Massoneria e i suoi ideali di libertà, uguaglianza e fratellanza*, «Chiesa viva», n. 537, p. 22.

> Adonai is also God by the eternal law, for there is no light without shadow, beauty without ugliness, and white without black. The absolute can only exist as two Deities: darkness is necessary for light to serve as a contrast, as the pedestal is necessary for the statue and the brake for the locomotive... The doctrine of Satanism is heresy; the true and pure philosophical religion is the faith in Lucifer, equal to Adonai, but Lucifer, the God of Light and God of Good, is fighting for humanity against Adonai, the God of darkness and demons.

In another passage from the previously mentioned *Morals and Dogma*, we read:

> The Christian, the Jew, the Muslim, the Buddhist, the follower of Confucius and Zoroaster can join as brothers and unite in prayer to the one God who is above all other gods.

This is the ecumenism that Pike theorized[88]: all religions are on the same level, and above all, there is the G.·.A.·.D.·.U.·., the true creative source of all religions. It is not necessary to be a theologian to understand that here, we are completely beyond the Christian horizon. When we then refer to the chivalric associations that

---

[88] Albert Pike, (2004), *Morals and Dogma.* (*wk. cited*). p. 153.

arose within the framework of Freemasonry and see these knights parading with crusader cloaks, crusader shields behind the *Beauceant*, we certainly cannot think that these individuals can be assimilated into medieval knights, including the Templars, ready to defend the Holy Land and Christianity at the cost of their lives.

Despite periodically holding cultural meetings, conferences, and debates on the topic of the Masonic origin from the Templar knighthood, it must be asserted, without fear of contradiction, that the two organizations have nothing in common, nothing to share.

Simply opening the Rule of the Order of the Temple, reading a few articles, and then comparing the content with the instructions and initiation ritual for the degree of Knight of the Sun or Prince Adept (XXVIII.·.), Knight of St. Andrew of Scotland (XXIX.·.), or Knight Kadosh (XXX.·.) allows one to understand that they are two separate worlds, completely different and light-years apart.

To think that medieval operative Masonry, that of cathedral builders, the art of Gothic architecture, had within it Templar knights, penitent soldiers who had taken vows of poverty, obedience, and chastity, seems like a significant stretch. It should not be forgotten that in that era, knights were all of noble lineage and were not inclined to manual labour or to assimilate with stonemasons and builders.

On the contrary, medieval operative Masonry was a guild that brought together skilled construction workers (masons, carpenters, stonemasons, etc.) to protect the specificities of their work and art, in addition to functioning as a mutual aid society, defending orphans and widows resulting from workplace accidents. It was present in various regions of Europe, mainly where significant works were set up, such as the construction of cathedrals. Operative Masonry continued its activities independently of whether the Templars, after the trial in Paris, had fled from France to seek refuge in Scotland or not.

Today, it seems truly unsustainable, given the absence of documents proving otherwise, to assert that Freemasonry is the heir of the Templar knighthood. This is not only due to the lack of concrete evidence but also because it is challenging to argue that a chivalric order named *Militia Christi,* composed of penitent Christian knights, could have given rise to an organization interested in esoteric studies and capable of evolving in a deistic, relativistic, anti-clerical, and antidogmatic direction.

The release of the current Code of Canon Law, after a 66-year process, was met with keen interest, especially in secular circles. There were great expectations that the Holy See would show openness toward participation in Freemasonry. The Grand Masters of the G.:.O.:.I.:., Virgilio Gaito and Gustavo Raffi, had put considerable effort into softening the anticlerical positions that had always been a distinctive feature of Italian Freemasonry.

The articles of the new Code of Canon Law that

concern us are fundamentally two. The first is found in Book VI - Sanctions in the Church - Part II, Title I, *Offenses Against Faith and Unity of the Church* [Can. 1364 - § 1]:

> Can. 1364 - § 1. The apostate, the heretic, and the schismatic incur excommunication *latae sententiae*[89], without prejudice to the provisions of can. 194, § 1, no. 2; a cleric can also be punished with the penalties mentioned in the can. 1336, § 1, nos. 1-3.

The second relevant article in the new Code of Canon Law is in Part II, Title II, *Offenses Against Ecclesiastical Authorities and the Exercise of Functions* [Can. 1374]:

> Can. 1374 - Whoever names an association that conspires against the Church shall be punished with a just penalty; and whoever promotes or directs such an association shall be punished with interdict.

Since the new Canon Law did not explicitly mention the imposition of excommunication on Freemasons, this raised many questions: did a Freemason fall under one

---

[89] The term '*latae sententiae*' indicates that excommunication takes effect ipso facto, meaning by itself, even without a declaratory intervention from the ecclesiastical authority.

of the three categories subject to excommunication or not? In the case that a Catholic belonged to Freemasonry, how should they be considered? An apostate? A heretic? Would excommunication be imposed because of apostasy, heresy, or being a Freemason? Essentially, reading the two articles of the new Canon Law did not clarify whether a Catholic could belong to Freemasonry.

The Code did not explicitly mention 'Freemasonry' but generally referred to associations that 'conspire against the Church[90].' The fact that, even without explicitly stating the abolition of excommunication, the word 'Freemasonry' did not appear anywhere in the text led the Masonic world to rejoice. This was also fuelled by reassuring news from the Catholic world overseas. In the lodges, it was strongly asserted that there were no longer obstacles for Catholics to join Freemasonry since the penalty of excommunication had been abolished. However, in 1983, the *Declaration on Masonry* from the Congregation for the Doctrine of the Faith, signed by the then prefect, Cardinal Joseph Ratzinger, and also endorsed by Pope John Paul II, came. This document, binding for all believers, explains the doctrinal reasons that make membership in both spiritual chivalry and

---

[90] For further reference, the relevant section in the Code of Canon Law is in Book VI, Sanctions in the Church, Part II, Penalties for Individual Offenses, Title II, Offenses Against Ecclesiastical Authorities and the Freedom of the Church (Canons 1370 - 1377). URL: *https://www.vatican.va/archive/cod-iuris-canonici/ita/documents /cic_libroVI_1370-1377-it.html*. (*Verified 27/08/2022*).

Freemasonry incompatible.

The document not only reiterated the historical position of the Catholic Church regarding Freemasonry but also affirmed that individual bishops could not modify the decision made by the Holy See. In a democratic country like Italy, no one could prevent Freemasonry from continuing to assert that there were no restrictions for Masons attending the Catholic Church. Similarly, no one could prevent the Holy See from stating that Masons were not part of the ecclesial community and could not access the Eucharist, being excommunicated.

On February 23, 1985, *L'Osservatore Romano*[91] published an unsigned article[92], commonly believed to be authored by then-Cardinal Ratzinger. The author took a firm stance in that piece, and many still wonder if and to what extent this uncompromising position against Freemasonry was the reason for the fierce attacks he later faced during his tenure as Pope.

The article aimed to clarify the reasons behind the pronouncement of the Prefect of the Congregation for the Doctrine of the Faith, stating that the Catholic faith and the Masonic method remained incompatible:

---

[91] *L'Osservatore Romano* is an official newspaper of the Holy See; it provides news, speeches, and official statements from the Pope and the Holy See, as well as articles on religious, ethical, cultural, and social issues.

[92] Osservatore Romano, 23-02-1985. *Riflessioni ad un anno dalla Dichiarazione della Congregazione per la Dottrina della Fede.*

> Regarding the statement on the incompatibility of principles, however, it is now argued that the essential aspect of Freemasonry is precisely not imposing any 'principle.' This refers to a philosophical or religious stance that binds all its members but rather brings together, beyond the boundaries of different religions and worldviews, individuals of goodwill based on humanistic values that are understandable and acceptable to all[93].

In essence, in the 1985 note, the author emphasized how inappropriate it was to speak of the incompatibility of principles, as Freemasonry's essential nature was not to impose any 'principle.' According to the author, this 'essential' characteristic made Freemasonry incompatible with the Christian faith.

> Even though it is stated that relativism is not adopted as a dogma, the author argues that Freemasonry effectively promotes a relativistic symbolic conception. Therefore, the relativizing value of such a moral-ritual community, far from being eliminated, is, on the contrary, decisive[94].

The observations of the author continue:

---

[93] *Ibidem.*
[94] *Ibidem.*

> Even when, as already mentioned, there is no explicit obligation to profess relativism as a doctrine, the relativizing force of such a fraternity, by its intrinsic logic, has the capacity to transform the structure of the act of faith so radically that it becomes unacceptable to a Christian «to whom his faith is dear» (Leo XIII)[95].

The expectations of the Masonic world, as well as many prelates strongly involved in the Second Vatican Council, were thwarted. Despite the great efforts made by the progressive faction, among them, we cannot forget Cardinal Achille Liénart, a member of the Council's Presidency, and Cardinals Döpfner, Frings, and König. Today, it matters little whether Cardinal Liénart[96] truly entered Freemasonry in his youth or whether he indeed reached the 30th degree (Knight Kadosh) of the Ancient and Accepted Scottish Rite in 1924. What truly counts is that he rendered a great service to Freemasonry with his intervention on the second day of the Council when, without being asked or granted permission, he spoke out. He demanded that the assembly reject all documents meticulously prepared by

---

[95] *Ibidem.*

[96] Achille Liénart (1884 - 1973) became a Catholic priest in 1907. Subsequently, he served as a professor of Sacred Scripture at the major seminary of Cambrai. From 1928 to 1968, he was the bishop of Lille, and from 1930, he held the title of cardinal in the Catholic Church.

the preparatory commissions.

Professor Enrico Maria Radaelli, in an article published in *Divinitas* (Year LVI, No. 3, 2013), addressing the 'break of conciliar legality' by Cardinal Liénart, seems to confirm the suspicion of many that it was an attempt to establish a conciliar church, ostensibly distinct from the Catholic Church and yet claiming to be such.

The Second Vatican Council, in addition to highlighting the presence of a progressive faction within the Church, also brought forth the figure of Bishop Marcel Lefebvre, who soon became the champion of conservatives. In a post-conciliar atmosphere characterized by modernism and grappling with the adaptation of liturgy and church structure, tensions arose between Monsignor Lefebvre and the Holy See.

On June 30, 1988, in Econe, Bishop Lefebvre ordained four bishops. The schism was consummated. Lefebvre and his community were excommunicated *ipso facto*, having placed themselves outside the Catholic communion. As the years passed, on Monday, April 18, 2005, Cardinal Ratzinger delivered the homily during the *Missa Pro Eligendo Romano Pontefice*. In his speech, he touched on a theme dear to him, relativism:

> While relativism, that is, letting oneself be carried 'here and there by any wind of doctrine,' seems to be the only attitude suitable for the current times. A dictatorship of relativism is forming that recognizes

> nothing as definitive and leaves only one's ego and desires as the ultimate measure[97].

The next day, after four ballots, Joseph Ratzinger was elected pope. He chose the name Benedict XVI, introducing himself to the gathered faithful in St. Peter's Square by defining himself as ‘a simple and humble worker in the vineyard of the Lord.’

Some considered Joseph Ratzinger as *the mild theologian from Tubingen*, while others saw him as *God's constable*. I believe that Pope Benedict XVI felt like a medieval knight who, having received a very challenging mandate, decided to embark on a mission with a lance in hand. His mission was to defend the authentic faith of the Christian people from the attacks of those who wanted to reduce the figure of Jesus Christ to an *avatar* or an Indian *guru*, attempting to turn Christianity into a super-religion, a kind of Organization of United Religions.

On January 21, 2009, the newspaper ‘l'Avvenire’ reported that Pope Benedict XVI had officially revoked the excommunication *latae sententiae* of the four

---

[97] The text *Missa Pro Eligendo Romano Pontifice,* 18 aprile 2005, Omelia del Cardinale Joseph Ratzinger, Decano del Collegio Cardinalizio, Patriarcale Basilica di San Pietro refers to the homily delivered by Cardinal Joseph Ratzinger, Dean of the College of Cardinals, during the Mass for the Election of the Roman Pontiff on April 18, 2005, at the Patriarchal Basilica of St. Peter. You can find the full text of the homily at the provided URL: *https://www.vatican.va/gpII/documents/homily-pro-eligendo -pontifice_20050418_it.html* (*Verified 20-12-2022*).

schismatic bishops ordained in 1988 by Mons. Lefebvre. To Bernard Fellay, Lefevre's successor, Ratzinger granted the restoration of the Tridentine Mass, which, for many believers, is the traditional Mass.

I don't believe it is a coincidence that Pope Benedict XVI, both on the day of his inauguration and on other occasions, always referred to himself as a 'simple and humble worker in the vineyard of the Lord.' The same metaphor is found in the famous papal bull of Pope Clement XII against Freemasonry, where the Holy Father promised to «watch day and night, like a faithful and prudent servant placed in charge of the Lord's household, so that this race of men does not plunder the house like thieves or ruin the vineyard like foxes[98]». The allusion to the role of a guardian protecting against Masonic infiltrations in the Vatican seems evident.

---

[98] Lettera apostolica *In Eminenti Apostolatus Specula*. (*wk. cited*). p. 183.

The Islamic Perspective on Freemasonry

Islam maintains a negative stance towards Freemasonry for various reasons. Chief among them is the belief that a Muslim should owe total obedience only to Allah, their Creator and Sole Protector. Muslims are guided by the Quran and the Sunnah of Prophet Muhammad as sufficient sources to lead their conduct and illuminate their path. Only these two truths deserve trust. A Muslim should never affiliate with any organization working for the destruction of their religion.

In theory, a Muslim could join service organizations like Rotary or Lions, but only if these organizations aim to expand Islam. It is neither suggested nor allowed to become part of associations like Freemasonry, which are openly sympathetic to Judaism. On this subject, the perspective of Sheikh Ahmad Kutty, a lecturer at the Islamic Institute of Toronto (Canada), is presented as follows:

> As far as I know, Freemasonry is a secret organization whose beliefs and practices are entirely kept confidential except to those who have been initiated. They have levels of secrets not disclosed to those at lower levels. A Muslim should never fall prey or pledge allegiance to something that the firm criteria of the Quran and the Sunnah cannot examine. Joining Freemasonry is like signing a blank check, accepting to unquestioningly pledge

> allegiance to an authority to comply with whatever desires they may have. No Muslim can unconditionally submit their will to anyone other than Allah. If someone does so, they are guilty of the most blatant violation, namely *shirk* (One who turns away from Allah). Allah says: 'They have other associates who prescribe them rules that Allah has not authorized.' (Ash-Shura: 21)[99].

Sheikh Kutty continues his discussion on the nature and operation of Freemasonry:

> Freemasonry is a secret organization with purposes that are never officially declared in public. It shrouds itself in secrecy to the extent that any new initiate makes a solemn oath not to reveal its secrets, being fully aware that disclosing these secrets will endanger its life.
>
> Admission to Freemasonry is not open to everyone. It recruits its members after a careful study of their characters and positions. It also strives to recruit among its members kings, presidents, ministers, prominent politicians, and highly influential

[99] Sheik Ahmad Kutty, *Can a Muslim Be a Freemason?* May 23, 2008, Islamic Board - Discover Islam - Connect with Muslims. URL: *https://www.islamicboard.com/general/134266987-can-muslim-becoming-mason.html*; translation by the Author. (*Verified 09-06-22*).

people. These individuals receive an honorary membership that keeps them on the fringes of society, meaning they do not participate in its decision-making process and are not made aware of its secrets.

Only those willing to work with dedication for the institution's purposes are made aware of these secrets. They must pass certain tests and be promoted to higher ranks in the Masonic hierarchy.

What attracts people to join Freemasonry is the assurance of mutual assistance that its members commit to provide at the time of joining. A Mason is expected to give unlimited support to other members of society. Members have some signs through which they recognize each other, such as the way they shake hands and certain symbols in their signatures, letters, etc. In countries where Freemasonry is well established, this can be of great advantage to any member showing dedication to the cause.

A certain number of people have written about the secret objectives of the Masonry. These were mostly former members who had left the institution after discovering that they could not reconcile with its objectives. Most of these cases occurred in countries where the society failed to promote itself, which, in turn, resulted in limited interest and membership. This led to some members quickly rising to higher ranks, allowing them to understand the secrets of Freemasonry better.

Through these individuals, we know that society has a very strict hierarchy that keeps members at a low level until they have passed a very severe test of loyalty and dedication.

It is now evident that Freemasonry serves the purposes of global Judaism and derives its name from that particular purpose. A 'mason' is a builder, and Freemasonry aims to rebuild the Temple of Solomon in Jerusalem. This will happen after the destruction of the Al-Aqsa Mosque because, according to Jews, the mosque was built on the site of the destroyed temple.

In essence, Freemasonry is interested in any activity that promotes the interests of Jews and advances their position in the world. The cover of absolute secrecy and its strict hierarchy allow the Masonic institution to exploit the positions and influence of its non-Jewish members to serve the Jewish cause.

It is interesting to understand that many of its members work for the Masonic institution, believing that they are solely serving the cause of freedom, equality, and justice. They remain completely unaware that they are actually serving the cause that will allow Jews supremacy in global affairs.

Over the years, Freemasonry has earned a series of enemies, particularly the Catholic Church. In light of these brief considerations, it must be clearly stated that if a Muslim joins Freemasonry, they contravene the teachings of Islam.

As mentioned earlier, the goals, policies, and practices of Freemasonry are contrary to the principles of Islam and violate its laws. For example, Islam believes in maintaining justice among all people, regardless of race, colour, family, social position, or creed. A Muslim must be fair to all people. Islam prohibits favouritism, nepotism, and discrimination on any basis. Masons favour each other based on their membership in the institution.

Islam respects other religions. Freemasonry, on the other hand, deceives its members into believing that they are promoting causes that will lead to the good and progress of humanity when, in reality, they are promoting the interests of those who seek to give Jews supremacy over all peoples of the earth.

Islam is the final message from Allah to humanity. It is the religion that replaces all past divine messages, including Judaism. Freemasonry seeks to destroy the Al-Aqsa Mosque to rebuild the Temple of Solomon in its place. How can a Muslim, then, become part of such a society?

Islam believes in open methods and declared objectives and orders its followers always to be sincere and follow the right path. Freemasonry wraps itself in secrecy to cover

> its evil practices. If its goals were truly to promote a better humanity, it would have come out in the open, declaring its objectives and policies to the world. Only evil cloaks itself in secrecy because it wants to hide its repugnant nature[100].

It is evident that the animosity and misunderstanding that exist between Jews and Muslims have been longstanding and involve religious, political, and social issues. Freemasonry is an additional battleground to the extent that the Islamic faithful see this institution as an arm of Judaism.

---

[100] *Ibidem.*

Catholic Church and Freemasonry: Foundations for Dialogue

Dialogue means to converse and initiate an open and frank discussion among individuals willing to sit at a table and reason democratically, without prejudices. The goals of dialogue are not to seek consensus at all costs or to demand that the other change their position. Instead, dialogue simply aims to increase mutual understanding, even though there might be a legitimate desire, sometimes from both parties or just one, for positions to come closer to the point of agreement.

In theory, this could happen, although it does not fall within the primary goals of dialogue. With the issuance of the encyclical *Ecclesiam Suam* on August 6, 1964, Pope Paul VI explained to the Christian people how a frank and serene dialogue with all people, even non-believers, was necessary for the Church. No one should be considered a subject without qualifications to receive the message of Christ. Only in this way could the Church fulfill its primary mission: the proclamation of the Gospel.

Great hopes arose in both the progressive Catholic world and Masonic institutions following the establishment of the Secretariat for Non-Believers on April 6, 1965. From the document *Dialogue for Non-Believers*, we present the introductory part in which the reasons for the Catholic Church's decision to engage in dialogue with non-believers are clearly explained.

In general terms, dialogue is understood here as any form of encounter and communication among individuals, groups, or communities with the intention of achieving either a greater understanding of the truth or improved human relations in an atmosphere of sincerity, respect for individuals, and with a certain mutual trust. Dialogue is particularly important and complex when established among individuals with different, sometimes opposing, opinions, aiming to dispel mutual prejudices and, to the extent possible, broaden their convergences, both in terms of simple human relations and in the pursuit of truth or for practical collaboration in various fields.

All these dimensions are present in various forms of dialogue.

However, since one or the other may play a predominant role, three fundamental types of dialogue can be distinguished:

- Encounter on the level of simple human relations, aiming to bring the interlocutors out of isolation and mutual mistrust, creating an atmosphere of greater 'sympathy,' mutual esteem, and respect.

- Encounter on the level of the search for truth, addressing questions of great importance for the individuals themselves, directing the joint effort toward a better understanding of the truth and a broader knowledge of things.
- Encounter on the level of action, which seeks to establish conditions for collaboration toward specific practical objectives despite potential doctrinal divergences.
- While it is desirable for dialogue to take place simultaneously in these three forms, each of them, in establishing an interpersonal encounter, retains its intrinsic value. Dialogue implies a certain reciprocity in the sense that each of the interlocutors gives and receives. It is thus distinguished from teaching, which is essentially ordered toward the disciple's formation through conversations with the master. However, dialogue, as it involves doctrinal enrichment for the audience present, constitutes a form of teaching towards them and also an implicit proclamation of the Gospel truth.
- The dialogue, as understood here, also differs from polemics and controversy since these are primarily oriented towards

> defending one's positions and demonstrating the error of others. Moreover, dialogue is not simply a matter of confrontation, as it must strive to bring the two parties closer and enhance mutual understanding. Finally, even though each interlocutor may legitimately aspire to persuade the other of the truth of their convictions, dialogue is not inherently aimed at this purpose but rather at a mutually enriching exchange[101].

After the Council, the Catholic Church, having declared its willingness to dialogue even with atheists, pondered the possibility of initiating a dialogue with Freemasonry. When the decision was made to establish connections with non-believers (i.e., atheists), a spontaneous question arose: how should Freemasons, in their various obediences and diverse identities, be considered? Should they be considered akin to non-believers?

To this question, Masonic scholars answered in the negative. Thus, the Catholic Church, given its long history of excommunications and relational difficulties

[101] "Dialogo per i Non Credenti" (Dialogue for Non-Believers), published by the Segretariato per i Non Credenti (Secretariat for Non-Believers) in Rome on August 28, 1968. URL: *http://www.cultura.va/content/cultura/it/pub/documenti/dialogonon-credenti.html* (*Verified 11/02/2022*).

with that institution, decided to entrust relations with Freemasonry to a new body dedicated to dealings with non-believers. In particular, this discreet and confidential task was assigned to Viennese Cardinal Franz König and Monsignor Vincenzo Miano, who was entrusted with the secretariat.

Before the Second Vatican Council, the climate between the two institutions was one of complete and mutual distrust. Father Rosario Esposito S.J. captures the atmosphere of those years well; on the one hand, there was the Masonic perspective:

> The Church has excommunicated us for two and a half centuries; it has even composed exorcisms against us. Why does it now want to dialogue with us? Does it want to convert us?[102]

On the other side, the sentiment of Catholics:

> These are people who have no desire to approach us; they will no longer be the Satanists of nineteenth-century polemics, but they are certainly not the ideal travel companions. No more wars, but everyone stays in their own homes. Why seek

[102] Esposito F. R., (1979), *La riconciliazione tra la Chiesa e la Massoneria. Cronaca di alcuni avvenimenti e incontri*, Ravenna, Italia, Longo, p. 7.

trouble?[103]

During that time, some, especially in the Masonic world, claimed that the Catholic Church was seeking dialogue due to its weaknesses. Even today, some argue that Christianity is on the decline, that churches are empty, seminaries are closing one after another, the faithful are old, there are no priests, etc.

However, we cannot forget that over these first two millennia, the Church of Rome has faced various aggressions, persecutions, heresies, schisms, and physical, theological, and doctrinal attacks. Especially in difficult times, the Catholic Church has known how to react. It has not been indolent, nor static, nor lacking in the ability for self-analysis. Suppose the Holy See continues to be a beacon of light, not only for Christianity but beyond. In that case, it is because of its capacity for reflection, for the openness of internal dialogue, for sometimes intense but necessary confrontation, to vigorously and resolutely follow the path laid out by the Lord.

We know that the positions of the Church and Freemasonry are extremely different, but thanks to the 'Pauline' spirit that pervaded the Second Vatican Council, dialogue became possible. Over seventy years had passed since the International Anti-Masonic Congress held in Trento in 1896, when some preliminary dialogues began from the bottom up,

[103] *Ibidem.*

primarily initiated by some progressive religious figures, mostly members of the Society of Jesus.

In the same period, scholars in history, sociology, philosophy, and politics began to question whether the hostilities between the Catholic world and Masonic institutions were justified or not. Gradually, the heated exchanges of opinions found in journals and essays gave way to a second phase in which, from reading texts, whether for or against, the focus shifted to the organization of meetings and conferences, where encounters between flesh-and-blood individuals replaced documents.

While the Secretariat for Non-Believers, recently established, held a progressive view and did not view unfavourably the abrogation of the canonical norm regarding the excommunication of Freemasonry, the Congregation for the Doctrine of the Faith (formerly the Holy Office), in 1981, opted for a decidedly strict position, namely the confirmation of the excommunication of Masons.

Both the progressive Catholic world and the Masonic world sought to identify the reasons why the Congregation for the Doctrine of the Faith had opted to maintain the excommunication. Among the reasons leading to this pronouncement, there was certainly the number of obediences, each with its particular vision. While some continued to hold anticlerical and antireligious positions, others were devoid of these connotations. There was also the issue that not all Masonic lodges were regular, meaning the United

Grand Lodge of England recognized them. The methods of swearing on the Sacred Book (usually the Bible) were not uniform and often unclear.

During those years, Monsignor Vincenzo Miano, Secretary of the Secretariat for Non-Believers, described the relations between the Church and Freemasonry as follows:

> They are not necessarily incompatible, and therefore, a Catholic who is such in faith and life can participate in the activities of the (regular) Lodge with a clear conscience because he knows that there will be no attack against his faith and moral convictions (for example, regarding abortion and divorce) and that he will not receive any pressure to act against his Christian conscience[104].

Miano then continued his thought by stating that non-Catholic members of a lodge cannot feel bound by the norms and dogmas of Catholicism.

> Freemasonry, as such, especially with its initiation practices and inherent symbolism, helps Catholic members and does not constrain them. It encourages and assists

---

[104] Esposito F. Rosario, (1979). *La riconciliazione tra la Chiesa e la Massone- ria. Cronaca di alcuni avvenimenti e incontri. (wk. cited).* p. 14.

> Catholic members who also desire to deepen their religious experience and moral life[105].

What can dialogue lead to? Certainly, it can result in collaboration in the social, welfare, and cultural fields. However, it cannot be ruled out that dialogue might lead to something more ambitious, such as shedding light on unclear aspects of Freemasonry, eliminating ambiguities and prejudices, and overcoming the feeling of distrust present on both sides. Referring to initiatory secrecy, the prelate states:

> But even in the more strictly doctrinal field and with absolute respect for the initiatory secret that every Mason rightly guards jealously, each of us can always learn something from dialogue with others: the dogma to which he adheres does not impede the Catholic; rather, faith, as it is not yet vision, implies a search (*fides quaerens intellectum*!). For this reason, we dialogue not only with Christians of other denominations in the search for the unity desired by Christ but also with Jews, Muslims, Hindus, and even with secular ideologies while excluding any possible syncretism. We believe that even in these religious faiths and ideologies, so different or even opposed, we can find positive elements

[105] *Ivi*, p. 15.

> and reasons to deepen our experience of faith. How could and should we not do the same with Freemasonry, given its especially Christian historical background?[106]

The Jesuit Monsignor Caprile, another member of that select group of priests who dared to engage in the Catholic/Masonic dialogue, asked: «Is it really impossible to be both a good Catholic and a good Mason?[107]»

To this question, he responded by providing the real motivations that led him to initiate the dialogue with Masonic institutions. The desire to dialogue with Freemasonry was not motivated by the intention to convert a Mason and bring him back to church for Mass, but:

> To ensure that within the lodges, respectful and observant of their most genuine original traditions, the faith and religious life of a Catholic brother (and similarly for other religions) are effectively respected and not hindered either ideologically or practically[108].

Among the various Masonic bodies currently operative, Monsignor Caprile wondered, which is the true Freemasonry, and which ones have deviated from

---

[106] *Ivi*, p. 15-16
[107] *Ivi*, p. 22
[108] *Ivi*, p. 14

the original path? The Catholic world needs Freemasonry to clarify certain points, such as the concepts of gnosis and secularism and the rejection of dogma; these three themes have always been subjects of dubious interpretation and sources of heated debates.

> [...] the fidelity (possibly a return) of Freemasonry to its original inspiration would be beneficial for all and would once and for all put an end to the incompatibilities and suspicions (sometimes more justified, sometimes less) that have prevented relations for over two centuries[109].

The progressive spirit, typical of members of the Society of Jesus, leads Monsignor Caprile to assert that dialogue with Freemasonry is fundamentally an act of justice. However, he acknowledges that dialogue is not without risks. It must be on equal terms and should not become, or even appear to be, «a beatification decree, nor an unconditional surrender, nor a submission to Canossa, nor a doctrinal compromise, or similar things[110]».

At this point, it is essential to highlight the thoughts of Giordano Gamberini, who, in 1979, held the position of the former Grand Master of the Grand Orient of Italy (Palazzo Giustiniani).

---

[109] *Ivi*, p. 23

[110] *Ivi*, p. 24.

In some pages titled *Mutual Respect*[111], the Grand Master recalls how, from 1738 to 1974, due to the excommunications received, Freemasonry was forced to recruit members, primarily among anticlerical individuals or those who had left the Catholic Church. In practice, Freemasonry found itself, albeit unwillingly, taking the place of the Church. The ghettoization and excommunications suffered by Freemasonry resulted in pushing the institution towards deviant alliances.

In the cited text, Gamberini believes that relying on the discourse of irregular or deviant Masonic bodies to maintain the excommunication was of little importance. The excommunication of 1738 was directed at original Freemasonry, not its deviations. In those years, the only three Grand Lodges in existence in Europe - the Grand Lodge of London, Scotland, and Ireland - had not undertaken hostile acts against the Catholic Church. Moreover, it should be noted that in a largely Protestant English Freemasonry, Catholics were admitted without facing any discrimination.

Gamberini cites 1974 as a particular year, the year of the end of excommunication. It should be remembered that on July 19, 1974, the Sacred Congregation for the Doctrine of the Faith (Cardinal Šeper) wrote a confidential letter to some Episcopal Conferences regarding the interpretation of Canon 2335 of the Code of Canon Law.

---

[111] *Ivi,* pp. 16-20.

In the letter, it was stated: «Canonical discipline is still valid, but where Masonic associations prove to be peaceful, that is, not openly fighting against the Church, this excommunication no longer exists». The document concluded: «It remains, however, forbidden in any case for clerics, religious, and also members of secular institutes to join any type of Masonic association».

This letter reached Cardinal Krol, President of the Episcopal Conference of the USA, who decided to make it public. For the Grand Orient of Italy's Freemasonry, these statements amounted to a triumph. It is noteworthy that on September 13, 1972, the United Grand Lodge of England recognized the regularity of the Grand Orient of Italy. From that document, the central passage is reported as follows: «The church no longer regarded Masonry as connected with satanism and atheism, and the position was one of mutual respect[112]».

The first attempts at dialogue between Freemasonry and the Catholic Church had originated in Europe in the 1930s through personal initiatives. In France, a friendship was established between the Jesuit Joseph Berteloot[113] and Albert Lantoine, who held the XXXIII degree of the Ancient and Accepted Scottish Rite and

---

[112] The Church no longer considered Freemasonry as connected to Satanism and atheism, and the position was one of mutual respect. Massoneria Italiana, Grande Oriente d'Italia, palazzo Giustiniani, September 13 1972, Recognition of the United Grand Lodge of England. URL: *https://www.docspopuli.it/fonti/Massoneria/Goi/riconoscimento-inghilterra_13-09-1972.pdf*. (*Verified* 10/10/2022.

[113] Berteloot J., (1952), *Jésuite et Franc Maçon*, Paris, France, Dervy.

was a member of the Grand Orient of France. Lantoine gained notoriety for authoring the *Lettre au Souverain Pontife*[114], in which he called for an end to the war between the two institutions, enabling both to combat atheist communism. Another Jesuit, theologian, and preacher, Father Michel Riquet, also worked towards the same goal.

The meetings in Bad Hofgastein in 1948 between the German Grand Master Bernhard Scheichelbauer and Cardinal Theodor Innitzer, Archbishop of Vienna, amounted to a total of five encounters.

In the United States, there were signs of progress. The participation of Cardinal Cushing in a banquet held by the Masons in Boston in support of J.F. Kennedy's presidential candidacy garnered particular interest.

In the Philippines, during Pope Paul VI's visit, the local Masonic organization welcomed him with a large mural on the road from Manila's airport to the city center. The mural expressed the Filipino Freemasonry's welcome to the Pope.

During the same period, the Scandinavian-Baltic episcopate decided that individuals affiliated with Freemasonry, seeking entry into the Roman Catholic Church, would not be required to renounce their membership in Freemasonry. With all these developments, by the mid-1970s, the end of excommunication seemed imminent.

---

[114] Lantoine A., 1937, *Lettre au Souverain Pontife*, Paris, France, Editions du Symbolisme.

After several years during which dual membership seemed to incur excommunication no longer, there were clear affirmations in Masonic lodges that excommunication had been abolished. Masons of the Catholic faith were explicitly informed that they were free to participate in religious services and receive the Eucharist.

Seven years passed, during which various episcopal conferences requested that decisions regarding dual membership be left at the diocesan level. Some surveys were conducted to assess the spiritual orientation and socio-cultural behaviour of various obediences. The results of these evaluations were not reassuring; except for sporadic cases, Italian Freemasonry was now devoid of the anti-clericalism of the Risorgimento era that had caused so much concern in the past.

On February 17, 1981, Cardinal Franjo Šeper, Prefect of the Sacred Congregation for the Doctrine of the Faith, froze the spirits of all those who had sought rapprochement between the two institutions and a resolution to the centuries-old conflict.

The *Declaration on the Adherence of Catholics to Masonic Associations*[115], concise and precise, removed any doubt. The excommunication had not been rescinded; it was still in force as stipulated by the current Canon Law; only the publication of the new Code could have changed the situation. Nevertheless,

---

[115] Declaration Regarding the Adherence of Catholics to Masonic Associations, p. 209.

throughout Italy, private meetings and public debates continued and continue today. One might wonder about the future of the relationship between the Church and Freemasonry. Certainly, both parties hope for a continuation of meetings and debates to increase mutual trust. It will be necessary to bring a good deal of goodwill, good faith, and charity to the table, as well as accepting and listening to each other.

The progressive component within the Catholic Church believes that much will depend on the role granted to local churches and dioceses in the Church/Masonry dialogue. As long as all decisions affecting world Freemasonry are made in Rome, the weight of past excommunications and disputes is likely to continue to hinder a more inclusive vision, which could be described as 'Pauline.'

Chivalry and Freemasonry are Irreconcilable?

The Holy See has consistently condemned the participation of Catholics in the ranks of Freemasonry. There are a total of 586 documents from the Magisterium in which the Church has urged the faithful to stay away from this association.

Why all this hostility towards Freemasonry? At first glance, this institution seems appealing. It is a worldwide organization with centuries of history; anyone can join, regardless of skin colour or social status. Even belonging to some Eastern religion or Islam does not pose problems. What matters is that the applicant declares a belief in God, as the institution is prohibited for atheists and unbelievers.

So far, Freemasonry seems to be just like any other service club, such as Rotary, Lions, Kiwanis, Zonta, etc., which engages in charitable initiatives while fostering interpersonal relationships. Perhaps there is just more secrecy.

In reality, it is not quite so: Freemasonry, in its three centuries of activity across various continents, has distinguished itself by promoting secularism and attempting to remove the Catholic Church from its role as a spiritual guide. In Italy, Freemasonry has been deeply involved in trying to suppress Catholic schools and eliminate religious teaching hours from schools. Furthermore, it has carried out intense political activities, starting from the years of the Risorgimento[116].

The Protestant pastor Anderson, in the chapter of the Constitution regarding duties towards God and Religion, stated in 1723 that 'a mason who understands the art well...never becomes either a stupid atheist or an irreligious libertine[117].'

While the prohibition for atheists to enter Freemasonry has always been an insurmountable obstacle explicitly sanctioned by the constitutions, over time, Freemasonry decided to undergo a radical change.

According to the operative Masonic tradition, a Mason was required to 'Practice everywhere the religion of the country[118].' Considering that the European population in the 18th century was predominantly of the Christian faith, ultimately, Masons were obligated to practice Christianity everywhere as the religion 'of the country.'

With the establishment of Speculative Freemasonry, a new vision began to take shape. It became functional

---

[116] The 'Risorgimento' represents a pivotal chapter, in Italian history, characterized by the desire to overcome fragmentation and foreign domination, particularly by Austria and other foreign powers. The term (can be translated 'Resurgence') refers to the 19th-century political movement for Italian unification.

[117] The Constitutions of Free Masons by James Anderson - 1723 Edition, p. 171.

[118] Eugenio Corecco, (1994) *La Chiesa e la Massoneria*, Conference at the Masonic Lodge 'Signa Hominis' in Lugano, November 4, 1994. URL: *https://www.eugeniocorecco.ch/scritti//scritti-pastorali/un-vescovo-e-la-sua-chiesa/ii-volume/chiesa-e-mondo-11/* (*Verified 07/10/2022*).

for Free Masonry that its adherents were devoted to a religion with which everyone agreed. From suggesting the practice of the country's religion, there was a shift to advocating for full personal freedom in matters of religion. Freemasonry would not prevent its members from following a more 'modern' religion, in step with the times, a rational, non-dogmatic religion.

We cannot forget that England was the stage for fierce struggles between Catholic and Orange factions. Choosing a religion based on rationality, non-denominationalism, and tolerance seemed Anderson to be an intelligent ploy to avoid aligning with one of the two political parties in question.

In the mid-18th century, the Grand Lodge of England, realizing that the Constitutions were causing problems, decided to ask the Protestant Reverend Entech to oversee a new edition of the Constitutions. Entech was established as the fundamental religious principle of Freemasonry, belief in God, defined as the *Great Architect of the Universe*, the observance of the Bible, and the humanitarian and philanthropic character of the institution.

However, French Freemasonry decided to take a different path. In Paris, among others, a lodge belonging to the Grand Orient de France, called 'le Nove Sorelle' (that is, Nine Sisters) was operational. It had, among others, notable figures such as Voltaire[119] and Benjamin

[119] Voltaire is the pseudonym of François-Marie Arouet (1694 - 1778). He was a French philosopher, writer, encyclopedist.

Franklin[120] on its roster.

The intellectual operatives in the lodge were particularly active in trying to give Freemasonry an anti-clerical turn, seeking to distance it as much as possible from Christianity.

It happened that, in 1877, the Grand Orient of France abolished the obligation for all Masonic brothers to believe in God; even the invocation of the Great Architect of the Universe became optional, and the rituals removed the phrase 'Freemasonry has as a principle the existence of God and the immortality of the soul[121].'

Due to these innovations, the Grand Orient of England and Germany decided to sever mutual recognition and reciprocity relations with French Freemasonry, which was declared irregular.

If the Masonic lodges on either side of the English Channel conflicted due to the figure and role of the Great Architect of the Universe, it must be emphasized that the god of Freemasonry was not and is not the god of Christians. The G.·.A.·.D.·.U.·. is the active principle of the universe, the one who puts order into cosmic

---

[120] Benjamin Franklin (1706 - 1790). He was an American scientist and politician.

[121] Le voeu n° IX, porté par les loges *La Fraternité Progressive* de Villefranche-sur Saône et L'Avenir de Paris, propose de supprimer «la croyance en Dieu» et «l'immortalité de l'âme». *Le convent de 1877, ses causes, ses conséquences*, André Combes, La Chaîne d'union 2017/3, n.81. URL: *https://www.cairn.info/revue-la-chaine-d-union-2017-3- page-38.htm* (*Verified 14/11/2022*).

chaos. Whether it was an initiatory symbol or an astral concept was intuited when Freemasonry decided to accept all existing religions.

Could the G∴A∴D∴U∴ be the same God as Christians, Muslims, Hindus, or Buddhists? No. The consequence of this vision was that the Masonic institution became a safe harbour, a destination for all those who believed in the divine conception of the G∴A∴D∴U∴ and recognized themselves in the dictates of the Anderson Constitutions.

The Mason is asked to be a 'free man,' free from beliefs, prejudices, blinders, superstitions, and dogmas. The Masonic brother must possess an open mind, be tolerant, ready and willing to seek the truth, the beautiful, the just, and enrich his knowledge.

So then, what are the reasons for this misunderstanding? Couldn't Freemasonry be an institution that brings man closer to God and spirituality? Is a first step capable of leading indifferent individuals to reflection? Could Freemasonry be able to bring its members closer to the Catholic Church? Or, on the contrary, does the fear prevail that Freemasonry might lead believers away from Christianity?

Could Freemasonry be the seat of true ecumenism, a place where members of different religious systems from distant cultures sit side by side to thank the common god, the Great Architect of the Universe?

At first glance, these considerations seem to slide away without causing wrinkles. Why not admit, then, that Freemasonry facilitates the approach to the Supreme Being? Couldn't Catholicism benefit from it?

The answer is no. Freemasonry cannot play the role of interreligious mediator because it is not a religion. Free Masonry has no theological doctrine, and since it is forbidden to speak of both politics and religion in the Lodge, this condition does not allow the creation and development of a Masonic theological doctrine. Furthermore, although endowed with its ritual, Free Masonry does not administer sacraments, has no relations with the sacred, and does not worship any god. Finally, it is not within the mission of Freemasonry to lead man to salvation.

The declaration of November 26, 1983, from the Congregation for the Doctrine of the Faith, is not ambiguous. We report a passage here:

> It has been asked whether the Church's judgment regarding Freemasonry has changed because it is not expressly mentioned in the new Code of Canon Law as in the previous Code. This Congregation is able to respond that this circumstance is due to an editorial criterion also followed for other equally unmentioned associations as they are included in broader categories. Therefore, the negative judgment of the Church regarding Masonic associations remains unchanged, as their principles have always been considered incompatible with the doctrine of the Church. Therefore, membership in them is prohibited.

> The faithful who belong to Masonic associations are in a state of serious sin and cannot access Holy Communion[122].

Freemasonry and the Chivalry of Christ belong to two different, distant, opposed, and irreconcilable worlds, and this has been the case for a long time. The former is an expression of a secularized secular culture; it is based on rational thought, humanism, and enlightenment. The latter belongs to a culture rooted in the Bible, the Gospel, and the saving mission of Jesus Christ.

In order to increase the level of knowledge and achieve a secular ethic, The Masons use reason and intelligence in a path that could be defined as a bottom-up growth process. On the contrary, the fullest realization of Christian life can only occur through the grace of God; certainly, we are called to collaborate, but it is the action of the Redeemer, the *primum movens*.

The journey of study and acquisition of new knowledge by the Mason, as well as the search for enlightenment, constitutes an unceasing process. After reaching what he considered the truth, soon another, truer truth will appear to the Mason's eyes in an unknown and mysterious process of continuous, relentless exploration.

---

[122] Declaration on Freemasonry - Congregation for the Doctrine of the Faith. - November 26, 1983, 211.

Freemasonry[123] claims to fight for freedom, to be against all tyranny and prejudice. The action is solely supported by rational thinking that manifests and materializes in free will, as understood by Giordano Bruno and other free thinkers. The institution believes that no principle can be imposed and vigorously opposes all dogmatism, even though it declares belief in a supreme being, which it names the Great Architect of the Universe.

It is evident that the God of Christians and the G.·.A.·.D.·.U.·. are not the same thing, as evidenced by the fact that in all Masonic rituals, there is no reference to Jesus Christ, the Holy Trinity, the Holy Spirit, Adam's sin, salvation, and resurrection. Free will is not a prerogative solely of Masons but also of Christians. Indeed, the God of Christians does not compel us to listen but speaks gently to the heart of each individual. It is then up to the individual to decide whether to follow Him or not.

Spiritual chivalry believes that at the origin of everything that exists and surrounds us, there is a good God. Being a Christian means adhering to a revealed religion, which involves a process of spiritual growth for the faithful, requiring an act of faith. This conversion cannot be completed without intervention from above. For the Catholic Church, consciences are awakened and

[123] The author refers mainly to the Freemasonry of the Grand Orient of Italy (G.·.O.·.I.·.) as Freemasonry, despite defining itself as Universal, presents significant differences among the various Orients.

illuminated by the transforming power of the Gospel.

> The mission of the Church, intended for all people of goodwill, is founded on the transformative power of the Gospel. The Gospel is Good News that carries within it a contagious joy because it contains and offers a new life: that of the risen Christ, who, by communicating his life-giving Spirit, becomes the Way, the Truth, and the Life for us (cf. Jn 14:6). It is the Way that invites us to follow him with trust and courage. In following Jesus as our Way, we experience the Truth and receive his Life, which is full communion with God the Father in the power of the Holy Spirit. It frees us from every form of selfishness and is a source of creativity in love[124].

Not all Masons are convinced, however, that Freemasonry is not itself a religion. Even if somewhat subdued, many Masons believe that Freemasonry is the true religion.

> Only Freemasonry possesses the true religion, which is Gnosticism. All other

---

[124] The mission at the heart of the Christian faith, the message of Holy Father Francis for World Mission Day 2017, October 22, 2017. URL: *https://www.vatican.va/content/francesco/it/messages/missions/documents/papa-francesco/20170604/giornata-missionaria.2017.html.* (*Verified 15/03/2022*).

> religions, especially Catholicism, have taken from Freemasonry what is true and incorporated it into their doctrines. They only possess absurd or false theories. The secret teaching of the supreme leaders of Freemasonry can be summarized in these words: establish all the rights of man... claim for man the possession of all these rights, the deprivation of which constitutes an usurpation against which every means, and every action is lawful[125].

Saint Thomas has clearly explained that there is an eternal law that emanates from God and the natural law is based on it. The Church operates with the aim of enlightening consciences and guiding them toward the good. Freemasonry, on the other hand, is different; it is an institution that speaks only to its adherents (the Brothers).

Initiation is the central premise of Masonic work. Its goal is the ethical refinement of man, achieved through the unveiling of secret knowledge, a result of an occult inheritance from past masters and sages.

There is a certain parallel between 'Christian initiation' and 'Masonic initiation.' The former transmits the words of Jesus and provides access to the

---

[125] Freemasonry, 1945, Florence, pp.18-21. A typewritten document consisting of 191 pages and intended for internal use. URL: *https://www.corrispondenzaromana.it/naturalismo-gnosi-in-un-testo-massonico-del-rsaa/* (*Verified 07/09/2022*).

first sacraments (Baptism, Confirmation, and Eucharist); the latter transmits and offers access to secret knowledge and esoteric rituals. With these tools, Freemasonry seeks to present to the Catholic believer the inconsistency of Christian initiation and, therefore, the sacraments received in early life.

That Freemasonry and Christianity, including spiritual chivalry, are irreconcilable is fully evident from the reading of the *Declaration of the German Bishops' Conference on the membership of Catholics in Freemasonry*. After six years of cordial meetings between the Grand Lodges of Germany and the German Bishops, the episcopate, in the concluding statement, noted:

> Even though Freemasonry, following the persecution during the Nazi era, has transformed greater openness to other social groups, its mentality, fundamental convictions, and 'work in the temple' have remained fully the same. The identified oppositions touch the foundations of Christian existence. Thorough examinations of Masonic rituals and the ideal Masonic world make it clear that contemporary membership in the Catholic Church and Freemasonry is excluded[126].

---

126 Declaration of the German Episcopal Conference on Catholic Membership in Freemasonry. pp. 193-208

Albert Lantoine, who in the early 1900s was a member of the 'Supreme Council of France of the R.·.S.·.A.·.A.·.' and later Grand Master of the G.·.O.·.F.·., stated: «Freemasonry is the only human religion[127]». In 1937, in a letter sent to the Supreme Pontiff, Lantoine expressed himself thus:

> I admit it, possessed as we are by the spirit of examination, we are the servants of Satan. You, holders of the truth, are the priests of God. These two Masters complement each other. They need each other. You push Power to exterminate Freemasonry. Beware! On that day, according to the expression of Meleager, you trumpets of death, 'you will burst into tears' because the death of Satan will mark the agony of your God[128].

Indeed, Freemasonry views religion with a naturalistic and rationalistic perspective.

> The traditional principle of Operative Freemasonry, according to which the Mason had to 'practice everywhere the religion of

---

[127] *Christianity and Freemasonry: an impossible equation?* Agnès Pinard Legry, 26-02-2018, Aleteia. URL: *https://aleteia.org/2018/ /02/26/christianity-and-freemasonry-an-impossible-equation/ (Verified 15/03/2022).*

[128] Lantoine Albert, Letter to the Sovereign Pontiff. (*wk. cited*). pp. 169-170.

> the country' in practice, Christianity, was replaced with one stating that it was more appropriate not to impose 'another religion, other than that in which everyone agreed,' leaving 'each one fully free on his personal opinions.' This meant introducing the idea of a purely rational and unrevealed religion, creating a fracture between the Masonic religion and the personal beliefs of its members. In this transformation, there was a clear attempt both to address, based on rationality, non-denominationalism, and a spirit of tolerance, the divisions created by the Protestant Reformation and to detach Freemasonry from Stuart Catholicism, integrating it into Anglicanism. To remedy the materialistic and irreligious doctrinalism into which the new speculative Masonry had quickly fallen, spreading across all the major countries of Europe, reaching India and the USA within just 20 years, the Grand Lodge of England, in the mid-18th century, commissioned a new edition of the Constitutions[129].

Clearly, the religion 'in which everyone agrees' is not Christianity but, in Anderson's vision, a purely natural religion. The definition of the Grand Architect of the Universe, the G∴A∴D∴U∴, does not provide us

---

[129] Corecco E., lecture: *The Church and Freemasonry*. (*wk. cited*). p. 2.

with the figure of a defined god but rather a container in which everyone can place their conception of a god that pleases them. We could say that the G.·.A.·.D.·.U.·. is a *do-it-yourself* god.

The Christian view is decidedly different, and the gap between the two conceptions of God is so wide that it is not possible to conceive of dual membership and a dual belief. It becomes difficult to think of a subject who feels, at the same time, both of these conceptions. The Christian God is personal, revealed to humanity, and became man in Jesus, the Nazarene; He descended to earth to fulfil a mission of redemption for which He gave His life. His death on the cross has taught us that death can be overcome; one can be reborn to enjoy an eternal reward in Paradise.

Of course, Freemasonry has a completely different view of religion since our Lord Jesus Christ would be nothing more than one of the many free spirits (avatars) appearing cyclically on Earth, as indicated by other religions. Therefore, Jesus Christ would not be the only begotten Son of God. The Masonic vision tends to discredit the Catholic Church, reducing it to an organization deprived of the cornerstone of faith, thus becoming a 'Christianity without Jesus Christ.'

With this operation, Freemasonry seeks to downgrade Christianity to the level of shamanism, a mythological religion, a superstition. Rational thought, enlightenment, and science itself are the means advocated by Freemasonry to free humanity from the yoke of false morality and false religion.

The true purpose of Freemasonry is to create a new society, made up of new men, in a new world order. If you will, it is an alchemical operation where, in a modern crucible, ethnicities, cultures, traditions, and religions are fused to obtain that 'tepid water,' that religion that suits everyone a little. This is why Masonry and Christian Chivalry are irreconcilable.

The Reasons for the Denial

There are various reasons why the Catholic Church has renewed, for all the faithful, including members of the spiritual knighthood, the denial to join the Masonic institution and also the many knightly groups that seemingly appear to be part of spiritual chivalry but, in reality, fall within the higher degrees of Freemasonry. There are several motivations for such a decision. Let's examine them:

- A Catholic Christian cannot be part of an organization that does not recognize any Church as the custodian of complete truth.
- A Catholic Christian cannot serve in an organization that advocates philosophical ideas and moral concepts contrary to Catholic doctrine.
- A Catholic Christian does not accept the Enlightenment and positivist vision, according to which spiritual and cultural growth depends solely on the guidance of reason.
- A Catholic Christian cannot be part of an institution that has, undoubtedly in the past, shown hostility and subversive activities towards the Holy See and Catholic doctrine.
- A Catholic Christian does not replace their God, the one who revealed himself in the Old and New Testaments, with the Great Architect of the

Universe (G.·.A.·.D.·.U.·.), an abstract, distant, and poorly defined entity.

- The G.·.A.·.D.·.U.·. cannot be identified with the Trinitarian God of Christians.
- A Catholic Christian cannot experience the full communion of Christian brotherhood if they have to consider a fellow Christian as 'profane' simply because they are not a member of Freemasonry.
- A Catholic Christian cannot live their relationship with God dually: on the one hand, a relationship of love with their heavenly father, operating on the plane of truth, justice, and love, and on the other hand, a relationship with a Supreme Being, distant and mysterious. A deity that observes without intervening.
- A Catholic Christian does not engage in paths of knowledge that go by the name of occult doctrines, including alchemy, magic, hermeticism, numerology, shamanism, Kabbalistic studies, Gnosticism, Martinism, spiritualism, etc.
- A Catholic Christian is not drawn to the 'free thought' practiced by Freemasonry, which believes that there should be no limits imposed on the pursuit of the just, the beautiful, and the true.
- A Catholic Christian cannot serve in an organization that does not accept the dogmas of

the Church.

After these necessary clarifications, let's now consider further reasons why the Catholic Church has expressed a negative opinion on the entry of its faithful into Freemasonry:

- Freemasonry aims to adopt a broader and more generous morality, freeing itself from what it perceives as empty, foolish ecclesiastical morality.
- Freemasonry has a syncretic vision, as in its rituals, there are evocations and symbols taken outright from the three Mediterranean monotheistic religions.
- In Freemasonry, enlightenment is granted in stages and at the end of an initiation rite officiated by a 'Master,' without the intervention of a higher spiritual entity.
- Freemasonry has a deistic conception that, by denying revelation, leads to a natural religion.
- Freemasonry promotes the creation of a 'new man,' the result of a blend of races, cultures, and religions. The theories underlying the melting pot are the same ones that, centuries ago, were the basis for the use of the athanor, the crucible used for alchemical transformations.
- Freemasonry believes that secular education is

the only one that serves the interests of modern society.

- Freemasonry has been excommunicated by the Church of Rome on various occasions, starting with the apostolic letter *In Eminenti*[130] by Pope Clement XII. This prohibition for Christians to engage in Freemasonry is still valid today.
- Freemasonry demands a high level of secrecy, or at least confidentiality, regarding its activities from its members; this is not required of Christian believers.
- Freemasonry imposes severe penalties on brethren who have violated the oaths taken during initiations or lodge activities. Even if these penalties are considered symbolic today, they are usually very serious, designed to instill fear and terror in the affiliates.
- In the higher degrees, Freemasonry is an instrument of strategies completely unknown to the base.
- Freemasonry claims not to be involved in politics or religion, but in reality, it has always been. Just think of the significant political action during the Italian Risorgimento... leading up to the P2 affair.

---

[130] In Eminenti Apostolatus Specula, pp. 183-188.

Reflections on the Bull In Eminenti Apostolatus Specula

The Catholic Church issued its first condemnation against the society of Freemasons in 1738 when Pope Clement XII issued the bull *In Eminenti Apostolatus Specula*[131]. Pope Clement XII was deeply concerned about the secretive nature of the organization. He highlighted that the members of the Masonic lodges were:

> Men of any religion and sect, content with a certain affected appearance of natural honesty... if they did not act wickedly, they would not so decisively hate the light[132].

It's essential to read this document with the mindset of the time. Ecumenism, the dialogue between religions, is a recent development for the Catholic Church. After centuries of rigidity, particularly since the Second Vatican Council, a new, more open-minded approach has emerged in the Church of Rome. Before then, anything outside the scope of Catholicism, especially if it was beyond Christianity, was viewed with extreme suspicion.

The Masonic movement found fertile ground

---

[131] In Eminenti Apostolatus Specula, pp.183-188.
[132] *Ibid,* p. 142

precisely in this extra-Catholic universe. It is no coincidence that the first constitutions of the Freemasons were drafted by a Presbyterian minister, James Anderson. After the Lutheran Reformation, while the Catholic Church pursued a strong unity of views and a dogmatic vision, the Protestant world embraced a pluralism of opinions, advocating an anti-dogmatic approach and allowing for broad interpretative freedom of the Scriptures. The fact that Freemasonry rooted itself in Protestantism was undoubtedly a factor that facilitated the proliferation of new obediences in subsequent periods.

The Church of Rome considers Freemasonry as a revised edition of the oldest heresy in the history of Christianity, namely, the heresy that attempted to undermine the foundations of the Church of Christ: Gnosticism. While in Christianity, salvation is bestowed through God's revelation, in Gnosticism (and Freemasonry), salvation results from human efforts to acquire knowledge. As is well known, the Church of Jesus Christ is a community open to all human beings, whereas Gnosticism (like Freemasonry) is a closed sect. Only the 'initiated' can attain enlightenment; others will continue to grope in darkness.

When Freemasonry embraces relativism, indifferentism, secularism, anti-dogmatism, and Gnostic thought, it has nothing to share with the community of Jesus's disciples; therefore, the excommunication that follows is certainly not motivated by trivial reasons.

Referring to the 'original sin,' we understand that

the Masonic vision depicts Adam as the man who decided to access the Tree of Knowledge. However, his attempt was not supported by the Creator but only by his presumption, the belief that he could become like God, relying solely on his strength. A similar situation occurred during the time of the Tower of Babel. This story tells us about those men who, solely through their efforts, sought to reach heaven to understand the language of God. Again, God became enraged in this instance.

The knight, like any Christian, realizes the significant place occupied by God in their life, not only in times of difficulty or pain but in everyday life. The story of Adam reminds us of the disconnection, the fracture that occurred with God as a result of that act. To mend that wound, the descent to earth of our Savior, Jesus Christ, was necessary.

> 'Indeed, God knows that when you eat of it, your eyes will be opened, and you will be like God, knowing good and evil.' Then, the woman saw that the tree was good for food, pleasing to the eyes, and desirable for gaining wisdom. So, she took some of its fruit and ate it, and she also gave some to her husband, who was with her, and he ate it. Then the eyes of both of them were opened, and they realized they were naked, so they sewed fig leaves together and made coverings for

themselves[133].

It is understood, therefore, how membership in a Freemasonic obedience and/or similar groups is an extremely serious matter from a spiritual perspective, as it is responsible for creating a new rift with God. After condemning the intrusion of Freemasonry into the house of God, plundering it, as thieves typically do, or ruining the vineyard, as foxes usually do, the pontiff briefly examines the key points that constitute an absolute impediment to Catholics joining Freemasonry:

a) Indifference and false ecumenism. The fact that individuals belonging to different sects and religions fraternize and gather under the name of a generic god, a Grand Architect of the Universe, jeopardizes the purity of the Catholic religion. In Catholicism, there is something peculiar, pure, and unique that must be preserved and cannot be shared with others. Freemasonry minimizes the truth inherent in the Catholic faith and promotes unity among individuals of any religion; one can speak of syncretism and indifference. The Catholic cannot be faced with a dilemma: either obey the precepts of the church or follow the indications of the Worshipful Master of the lodge.
b) Inviolability of secrecy. The work done in lodges is secret; meeting places are secret;

[133] Gen.:3, 5-7.

members are obligated to maintain an inviolable silence about the acts they secretly perform in the lodges. This suggests that there is fundamental dishonesty and a good deal of wickedness in Freemasonry, as the adepts love darkness and abhor light.

c) Oath on Sacred Scriptures. Due to the solemn oaths and secrecy to which the adepts are bound, it is not easy to understand the real purposes of these Freemasonic sects and whether they conspire only against the Church or also against the State.

d) Opposition to sanctions. These societies oppose civil sanctions as much as canonical ones and continue to gather despite the necessary authorizations. It should not be overlooked, the Pope notes, that in many countries, the mentioned societies and associations have already been proscribed and banned by laws of secular princes[134].

Clement XII felt it necessary to intervene, prohibiting members of the Catholic Church from belonging to Freemasonry, as Catholics see those who join Freemasonry as heretical, perverse, and blasphemous individuals. Belonging to Freemasonry means living in mortal sin, leading a scandalous life, and constituting a current danger to the spiritual life of

---

[134] During the period when the Pope promulgates *In Eminenti Apostolatus Specula*, Freemasonry is banned in the Netherlands, while facing significant issues in Spain, Portugal, France, and Italy.

others. The pontiff is seriously concerned about the damage that Freemasonry could cause, both politically and spiritually. From these considerations arises his need to 'watch day and night, like a faithful and prudent servant placed in charge of the Lord's household[135].'

The Pope expects that no one will favour the aforementioned societies of Freemasons. He warns that all Freemasonry members, as well as supporters and sympathizers, will incur excommunication, which will occur *ipso facto*, without any official communication. The imposed penalty must be valid in perpetuity, and no one can be absolved, except at the point of death, by anyone other than the Roman Pontiff *pro tempore*.

After urging bishops, prelates, and inquisitors to prosecute transgressors in every case and everywhere, the Pope reminds us that these individuals must be repressed with the same penalties with which suspects of heresy are struck. If necessary, inquisitors should seek the help of the secular arm.

> Therefore, let no one absolutely be allowed to violate or, with daring audacity, contradict this page of Our declaration, condemnation, command, prohibition, and interdiction. If anyone should dare to do so, let them know that they will incur the wrath of Almighty God and the Holy Apostles Peter and Paul[136].

---

[135] The apostolic letter (Bull) *In Eminenti Apostolatus Specula*, Supreme Pontiff Clement XII, p. 144.

[136] *Ivi*, p. 147.

This occurred about three centuries ago. Today, of course, many things have changed in society and the Catholic Church; however, the excommunication towards Freemasonry remains.

On Excommunications

It is the practice of esotericism that seals the deep divide between the two institutions. Indeed, Masonic knowledge is not accessible to everyone; it is not 'in the light of day' but, on the contrary, is available only to a restricted circle of individuals co-opted to be part of it. The Church of Christ does not appreciate this mode of operation. Christianity is accessible to all those who wish to know it. Christian doctrine has always been public, available, and free. There is no secret; esoteric Christianity is reserved for members of some clubs. Everyone can access the Old and New Testament, encyclicals, liturgical rituals, documents of various congregations, etc.

On this statement, we must pause for a moment. In the view of Protestants, Masons, and anticlericals, this would not correspond to the truth. In their vision, the Catholic Church would be a cunning, obscurantist organization, stifling 'free thought' by always preventing and prohibiting the free reading of the Sacred Scriptures, especially the Bible. This view would be supported by two concrete facts: the acts of the Council of Toulouse and the creation of the Index of Prohibited Books. Here is what the Council of Toulouse established in 1229:

> We forbid any layperson to possess books of the Old or New Testament translated into the vernacular. If a pious person desires it, they

> can have a Psalter or a Breviary... but in no case should they possess the aforementioned books translated into the Romance language[137].

It is evident that the prohibition of the Council of Toulouse did not refer to the reading of the Bible, as one would like to believe, but only to the translation of the text in vulgar language. It should be remembered that, in those years, in the south of France, heretical movements (Cathars and Albigenses first and foremost) were present, which provided Gnostic and heterodox interpretations of the Sacred Scriptures. For this reason, the Holy See decided to allow the reading of translations in the vulgar language, starting with the translation into Latin by Saint Jerome (the so-called *Vulgate*[138]), only in cases where these translations had obtained the official approval of the Holy See.

As for the Index of Forbidden Books, it should be said that many texts not approved or decidedly contrary

---

[137] La Chiesa e la proibizione della lettura della Bibbia, December 29, 2017. URL: *https://luis-apologeticon.blogspot.com/2017/12/la-chiesa-e-la-proibizione-della.html* (*Verified 11/09/2022*).

[138] The term *Vulgata* refers to the Latin translation of the Bible carried out by St. Jerome towards the end of the 4th century. The name *Vulgata* is derived from the Latin *vulgatus*, which means 'made common' or 'common'. St. Jerome undertook this translation based on the ancient Greek and Hebrew versions of the Bible with the aim of making the sacred text accessible to the common people. The *Vulgata* became the official version of the Bible for the Catholic Church for many centuries and has been widely used in liturgical and theological contexts.

to Christian doctrine were included in this list. In the Index, there were more than forty translations of the Bible in vulgar language.

Various reasons explain why these translations were placed on the index: in some cases, this depended on the fact that the translations were carried out by individuals with little theological preparation; other times, the inclusion in the index followed the fact that the translators were not of the Catholic faith. Although the idea of having books on the index generally triggers a sense of repulsion, we cannot deny that an institution like the Catholic Church had and still has the right to decide which, among the various publications that touch on themes of the Catholic Christian faith, were in line with traditional principles and which lacked these qualities.

To be frank, referring to Bible translations, it must be said that in many cases, it was not just translation problems but also issues of interpretation and extrapolation of concepts. In essence, some of these translations were heretical in the sense that they contested the role of the Church of Rome, temporal power, and questioned the sacraments, in addition to denying the corporeality of Christ and preaching an extremely ascetic way of life, a true departure from the world.

It was the Calvinist and Lutheran doctrines that prompted the Church of Rome to conduct a thorough, organic, and definitive analysis of Catholic dogmas. In December 1545, Pope Paul III opened the Council of

Trent.

Below are some decrees that were defined on that occasion:

> SESSION IV (April 8, 1546) First Decree: [...] And since the Synod knows that this truth and discipline are contained in written books and unwritten traditions, collected by the apostles from the mouth of Christ Himself and from the apostles themselves, transmitted almost hand in hand under the inspiration of the Holy Spirit, following the example of the Orthodox fathers, with equal piety and reverence [the Church, editor's note] accepts and venerates all the books, both of the Old and New Testament, for God is the author of both, and also the traditions themselves, which concern faith and morals, since they are considered dictated by Christ Himself orally or by the Holy Spirit, and preserved with continuous succession in the Catholic Church [...].
>
> Second Decree: The Vulgate edition of the Bible is accepted, and the method of interpreting sacred Scripture is prescribed [...]. The same sacred Synod, considering, furthermore, that the Church of God could derive no small benefit if it were known which, among all the Latin editions of the sacred books in use, should be considered authentic, establishes and declares that this same ancient Vulgate edition, approved in the

> Church by the usage of so many centuries, should be considered authentic in public readings, disputes, and preaching, and that no one should dare or presume to reject it with any pretext.
>
> Furthermore, to restrain overly presumptuous minds, it declares that no one, relying on their own wisdom in matters of faith and morals concerning Christian doctrine by twisting sacred Scripture according to their views, should dare to interpret it against the sense that the holy mother Church has always held and holds, to whom it belongs to judge the true sense and interpretation of Sacred Scriptures, or even against the unanimous consent of the fathers, even if these interpretations should never be published. Whoever contravenes this should be reported by the ordinaries and punished according to the law[139].

Christianity is a monotheistic religion whose followers believe in God, in Jesus Christ, His only Son, and the Holy Spirit. It recognizes Jesus Christ as the one who redeemed humanity from the sin of Adam, and after dying on the cross and being buried, He rose again.

Although the Edict of Milan in 313 had granted freedom of worship to Christians, from the 3rd to the

---

[139] I Decreti del Concilio di Trento, 8 aprile 1546, sessione IV. URL: *https://www.documentacatholicaomnia.eu/03d/1545-1563, concilium_tridentinum,_acta,_EN.pdf.* (*Verified 04/03/2022*).

5th century, followers of the Master decided to adopt a certain reserve towards neophytes. During that time, the Catechumenate was established, an institution tasked with preparing candidates for the sacrament of Baptism.

It involved a distinction in preaching and participation in the sacrifice of the Eucharist. Catechumens were not explained the sacred mysteries; they only received basic information about the Baptism ritual and key doctrines. Complete instruction, especially information about the Eucharist, was provided only after receiving Baptism.

The term *Disciplina Arcani* (discipline of secrecy) refers to the practice, prevalent in those years, of not discussing sacred rites and doctrines with outsiders. The Christian tradition of the early centuries, linked to contingent factors and later abandoned with the improvement of the political climate, cannot be equated with Freemasonry's desire to keep ceremonies, sacred words, step rituals, and initiation rites at various degrees hidden.

Christianity is the revelation of God's love, the announcement that all of humanity, without distinction of race, culture, or social status, can be saved. Resurrection and paradise are possible for all those who can undergo conversion. How can the assertion of John (14:6), Jesus said to him, 'I am the way, and the truth, and the life. No one comes to the Father except through me,' be reconciled with the Freemasonry approach, where no truth is considered final and absolute?

The condemnation of Gnosticism by the Church of

Rome occurred in the 2nd century, with the writings of Saint Irenaeus of Lyon[140]. Key reasons for this condemnation include the Gnostics' belief that the true God is not the Creator God but a higher God, an entity of pure essence and love.

Another reason is the Gnostic conviction that Jesus, during His earthly period, was not a flesh-and-blood man but only assumed a human appearance. Consequently, the crucifixion and resurrection could not have happened; His death would have been a mere fiction.

Gnostic thought is incompatible with Catholic Christianity, especially because members of this sect have always claimed that Gnosticism originated from Jesus Himself. According to them, the Master delivered secret teachings to His disciples, making the Gnostics the custodians of occult knowledge, a true esoteric Christianity to be revealed only to initiates of these mysteries.

Despite efforts by popes and entities dedicated to defending the Catholic faith, Gnostic thought, officially confined between the 1st and 4th centuries after Christ, continued to operate through Martinism. Marsilius (pseudonym of Vincenzo Soro, the Mason of Ozieri considered the leader of the Gnostic Church in the early 20th century) wrote in 1922:

---

[140] San Ireneo di Lione, (2009), *Contro le Eresie*, Roma, Italia, Città Nuova.

> There will not be, as there are today, a hundred or two hundred rival Churches, but the Great Universal Church of all men gathered in the Unique Religion, and One who hides under different cults amid the dogmatic formulas of various religions[141].

The figure of Saint Irenaeus of Lyon, a staunch fighter against Gnosticism, despite his theological activity spanning the first and second centuries AD, remains relevant and serves as a bridge between Eastern and Western Christians. Recently, Pope Francis declared him a Doctor of the Church with the title of 'Doctor unitatis,' almost emphasizing how much the Church still needs him and a unified and ecumenical vision.

Now, it is no secret to affirm that Freemasonry, even today, practices esotericism and is closely related to Gnosticism, Martinism, and alchemy. The institution of Freemasons offers its followers the opportunity to progress within the lodges through the acquisition of occult knowledge, the 'masonic science.' After overcoming a long series of initiation rituals, as they advance in the initiatic path, followers are told that they can achieve a higher state of consciousness, thus attaining full self-awareness and ultimate realization. None of this has anything to do with Christianity.

Since 1738, excommunications towards Freema-

---

[141] Vincenzo Soro, (1922), *La Chiesa del Paracleto. Studi sullo Gnosticismo*, Todi, Italia, Atanòr, p. 92.

sonry have followed. Initially, as a response to the strong anti-Catholic spirit of that institution, and later for social, civil, and political reasons; indeed, the Church believed that Freemasonry not only aimed to destroy Christianity but also to subvert society as a whole. The intention to prohibit Catholics from any form of involvement or proximity to Freemasonry, first expressed by Pope Clement XII, was later renewed and confirmed on May 18, 1751, by the bull *Providas Romanorum* of the Supreme Pontiff Benedict XIV[142].

With this document, Pope Benedict XIV explicitly confirmed that the condemnation against the society of Free Masons, promulgated by his predecessor, was perpetual. The prohibition applied to all Christians. Excommunication was imposed not only on the members of Freemasonry but also on those who worked in their favour, providing support, assistance, protection, and hiding for the 'brothers.'

Providas Romanorum addresses the controversy that arose regarding the validity of the excommunication. In the Masonic world, it was argued that Clement XII's excommunication was not valid because it was not confirmed. Benedict XIV expresses his astonishment at the superficiality of this consideration since papal constitutions have never

[142] Benedict XIV, born as Prospero Lorenzo Lambertini on March 31, 1675, in Bologna, Italy, was indeed a prominent pontiff of the Catholic Church. He was elected Pope on August 17, 1740, and served until his death on May 3, 1758. Benedict XIV was the 247th pope in the history of the Catholic Church.

needed explicit confirmation by a successor.

Although it was clear that a document like *In Eminenti* did not require any confirmation, due to the presence of liars and slanderers capable of devising a thousand subterfuges and finding a thousand loopholes, Benedict decided to adopt Clement XII's thinking and show the same firm will as his predecessor in condemning Free Masonry.

To seal the full harmony of intentions and operational continuity with Clement XII, Benedict decided to include the bull *In Eminenti Apostolatus Specula* in its entirety in the bull *Providas Romanorum*. This operation dispelled any doubts about the real intentions of the pontiff.

As clearly indicated by his predecessor, the excommunication of Christians/Masons could only be lifted by the pope. A year had passed since the Jubilee when the pontiff, never forgetting the virtue of charity, decided to grant absolution to the many Catholics who had sincerely repented of joining Freemasonry.

As tradition required, Benedict XIV also decided to use the royal 'We' for the drafting of the bull; however, the pope emphasized that this mode of writing should not be interpreted as a mere adherence to the custom of the *pluralis maiestatis*. By using the royal 'We,' the pontiff was underscoring the perfect unity of intentions with his predecessor.

The bull *Providas Romanorum* concludes by reiterating that no one will be allowed to violate or contradict the content of this document. In case anyone dared to do so, they would incur the wrath of Almighty God and the Holy Apostles Peter and Paul.

Seventy years had passed when, on September 13, 1821, Pope Pius VII[143] made public the bull *Ecclesiam a Jesu*. This document was addressed not only to Freemasonry but also to the Carbonari.

The bull begins by emphasizing how, for a long time, the Holy See had raised its voice against secret societies. However, despite various actions taken, these societies had not been intimidated at all and had, in fact, continued to thrive and expand. The papal letter was published in the year when insurrectionary attempts were manifesting across Europe against absolutist regimes. After Spain, revolutionary movements erupted in Italy, from Sicily to Piedmont. Nevertheless, the pope did not back down. Pius VII was a pontiff with solid theological foundations and a strong personality; he had already overcome the events of 1799, which occurred while he was in a conclave with his fellow cardinals, as well as the confrontation with Napoleon Bonaparte[144].

---

[143] Pope Pius VII, born as Barnaba Chiaramonti, indeed served as the 250th pope, with his pontificate spanning from 1800 to 1823. He was born on August 14, 1742, and he passed away on August 20, 1823.

[144] The phrase *Non debemus, non possumus, non volumus* (We must not, we cannot, we will not) was indeed uttered in 1809 by Pope Pius VII in response to Napoleon's request. Napoleon wished to have all the territories of the Papal States ceded to the French Empire. Pope Pius VII's refusal with this statement led to tensions

In his roles as Shepherd and King, he decided to address the Carbonari directly, one of the secret societies that used and often abused the symbols and signs of Christianity.

The Holy See certainly possessed the rituals and doctrine of the Carbonari and was well acquainted with the *Alta Vendita* as the entire pyramid of various secret societies. In the rituals of the first degree and the Carbonari catechism, Jesus Christ was referred to as the Ruler of the universe. As one progressed up the hierarchical scale of the Carbonari, the symbols inherent to Christianity transformed, becoming a metaphor for the rebellion against absolute power.

Pius VII was confident that at the root of the revolutionary movements erupting throughout Italy, the Carbonari doctrine played a crucial role. Therefore, after outlining the main errors of Carbonari thought and empha- sizing the dangerous nature of that doctrine as the principal cause of revolu- tionary movements, the pope sought to invoke the bulls of his predecessors and the edicts through which he himself had made his voice heard.

The Pontiff decided to refer to both the edict of the Secretariat of State dated August 15, 1814 - a document that, in turn, referred to a proclamation issued under the magistracy of Clement XII and published on January 14, 1739, by the Secretary of State Cardinal Giuseppe

---

between the Catholic Church and Napoleon. It eventually escalated to the arrest of Pope Pius VII by Napoleon's forces in 1809.

Ferras - and the allocution *Optatissimus Tandem* of September 26, 1814. From this latter allocution, we quote a passage:

> Indeed, as soon as we broke free from the impious captivity that held us back, we returned to our duty, as you know, to diligently work towards understanding and healing the ills of the Church. We dispersed, within the Pontifical State, the secret sects of wicked men, fierce enemies of Religion and the thrones of Princes[145].

In the following years, the Papal Throne saw the succession of Pope Leo XII, Pope Pius VIII, Pope Gregory XVI, Pope Pius IX, and Pope Leo XIII.

Pius IX[146] was one of the longest-reigning popes and arguably one of the most determined figures in papal history. On the topic of Freemasonry and secret societies, he delivered the allocution *Multiplices Inter*[147]

---

[145] Allocution *Optatissimus Tandem* ('Finally the Most Desired'), September 26, 1814, Supreme Pontiff Pius VII. URL: *https://www.vatican.va/content/pius-vii/it/documents/allocuzione-optatissimus-tandem-26-settembre-1814.html* (*Verified 19/09/2022*).

[146] Pope Pius IX, born as Giovanni Maria Mastai-Ferretti, served as the 255th pope of the Catholic Church, but his pontificate spanned from 1846 to 1878. He was elected pope on June 16, 1846, and remained in office until his death on February 7, 1878.

[147] Allocuzione *Multiplices Inter* ('Among the Many'), September 25, 1865, Supreme Pontiff Pius IX. URL: *https://www.vatican*

(September 25, 1865) and the encyclical *Etsi Multa Luctuosa*[148] (November 21, 1873). Reading a passage from *Etsi Multa Luctuosa* helps us understand the tone of the encyclical:

> Some of you, Venerable Brothers, might be surprised at the extent to which the war waged against the Catholic Church is expanding today. However, anyone who knows the character, objectives, and purpose of these societies, whether they be called Masonic or by any other name, and compares them with the character, method, and scope of this war by which the Church is attacked from almost every side, will undoubtedly not doubt that this calamity must be attributed to the schemes and machinations of these societies. For from them is formed the synagogue of Satan, which marshals its army against the Church of Christ, raises its banner, and comes to battle.

Leone XIII[149] was among the popes who exerted

.va/content/pius-ix/it/documents/allocutio-multiplices-inter-25-septembris-1865.html (*Verified 19/09/2023*).

148 Allocuzione *Etsi Multa Luctuosa* ('Although Many Sufferings'), November 21, 1873, Supreme Pontiff Pius IX. URL: *https://www.vatican.va/content/pius-ix/it/documents/enciclica-etsi-multa-21-novembre-1873.html (Verified 19/09/2023).*

149 Pope Leo XIII, born Vincenzo Pecci, served as the 256th pope of the Catholic Church from 1878 until his death in 1903. Pope Leo XIII was born on March 2, 1810, and he became pope on February

considerable efforts against Freemasonry. Notable encyclicals on the subject include *Humanum Genus* (1884), *Officio Sanctissimo* (1887), *Dall'Alto dell'Apostolico Seggio* (1890), *Custodi di Quella Fede* (1892), *Inimica Vis* (1892), and *Praeclara Gratulationis* (1894).

The *Humanum Genus*[150], beginning with a recall of humanity's rebellion against God, describes the birth of two perpetual warring factions. One, from the beginning, struggles for the triumph of good, while the other, from the beginning, works for the triumph of evil. Those who choose to belong to the former must serve God and His only-begotten Son with all their minds and hearts. Those who align with the latter are those who refuse to obey the eternal and divine law and work for the advent of Satan's kingdom.

The battle between good and evil has persisted for time immemorial. However, the Pope asserts that today, the supporters of evil have gained strength as they have

---

20, 1878, remaining in office for over two decades until his passing on July 20, 1903.

[150] *Humanum Pauca Vivit Genus* is an apostolic letter written by Pope Leo XIII, issued on April 4, 1889. The title can be translated as 'The Human Race Lives Scarcely a Little While'. This document addresses the condition of the working class and the social order, discussing the rights and duties of workers and the principles of social justice. It is a clear condemnation of the philosophical and moral relativism of Freemasonry; April 20, 1884. URL: *https://www.vatican.va/content/leo-xiii/it/encyclicals/documents//hf_l-xiii_enc_18840420_humanum-genus.html.* (*Verified 15/09/2022*)

found assistance from the Masonic institution. After conspiring in the shadows for a long time, the Masons are now openly playing their cards against the sovereignty of God, aiming to eliminate the figure of Jesus Christ, our Savior, from the world.

Leone XIII is confident that a war against Christianity is underway and deems it necessary to identify the enemies and resist their attacks. The *Humanum Genus* is an encyclical with a strong sociological connotation; it does not appear dated as it describes the moral effects of Masonic philosophy in a society increasingly indifferent and distant from religion. According to the Pope, Freemasonry aims to establish a new world order and, to achieve this, must destroy everything Christian in society.

> Our Roman Pontiffs, vigilant guardians for the welfare of the Christian people, soon understood who this formidable enemy was and what it aimed for, emerging from the dens of dark conspiracies. Anticipating the future, almost giving the signal, they warned princes and people not to be deceived by cunning and insidious plots[151].

In Freemasonry, which the Pope defines as a 'lethal disease,' a 'shadowy sect' with 'malevolent tendencies, false doctrines, and nefarious works,' Leone XIII sees

---

[151] *Ivi*, p. 2.

the personification of permanent revolution:

> In this pernicious and deceitful work, a shadowy sect advances ahead of the others, which society has been carrying in its midst for many years, like a lethal disease that contaminates its health, fertility, and life. A permanent personification of revolution, it constitutes a kind of inverted society whose purpose is a hidden dominance over the recognized society and whose raison d'être consists of waging war against God and His Church. It is not even necessary to name it, as everyone recognizes Freemasonry by these signs, which we specifically addressed in our encyclical 'Humanum Genus' on April 20, 1884, denouncing its malevolent tendencies, false doctrines, and nefarious works[152].

With these foundations, this history, and these documents, the Church of Rome reaches the Second Vatican Council.

---

[152] *Vigesimo Quinto Anno (*"Twenty-fifth year"), is an encyclical written by Pope Leo XIII, issued on March 19, 1902. This encyclical is subtitled "On the Function of the State," and it discusses the proper role of the state in relation to social justice and the common good. It emphasizes the importance of the state recognizing and respecting the natural rights of individuals. URL: *https://www.vatican.va/content/leo-xiii/it/apost_letters/documents/hf_l-xiii_apl_19020319_vigesimo-quinto-anno.html. (Verified 17/09/2022*).

Before concluding this chapter, it is necessary to provide the reader with a brief overview of Canon Law. Canon Law refers to the entire body of regulations specific to the Catholic Church. The first version was promulgated in 1917 by Pope Benedict XV (Pio-Benedictine Code). Articles 2335-2336 of the code stated:

> Those who enroll in Masonic or other societies plotting against the Church or civil authority incur excommunication reserved to the Apostolic See. Clerics who invade the freedom and rights of the Church beyond the penalties established will also be suspended or deprived of benefits, offices, dignities, pensions, or positions. If they are religious, they will be deprived of offices of active and passive voice, along with other constitutional penalties. If these individuals enroll in Freemasonry or similar sects, they will be reported to the Holy Office.

The publication of the new *Codex Iuris Canonici* (C.I.C. or 'Code of Canon Law') was anticipated not only in religious circles but also by all of civil society, especially by Masonic obediences. There were rumours that the new version was not just a revision of the Pio-Benedictine Code but a new formulation, a complete reform inspired by the conclusions of the Second Vatican Council.

After many meetings held in previous years and

confidentially, between authoritative representatives of the Church of Rome and the grand masters of Austrian and German Freemasonry, international Masonic lodges looked with confidence to the Holy See. The hope was that membership in the Masonic institution would no longer be considered a reason for excommunication. Information from the Congregation for the Doctrine of the Faith had leaked, raising optimism about the removal of the prohibition; it seemed that excommunication would be lifted, provided that Catholics only joined regular lodges.

On January 25, 1983, sixty-six years after the previous version, Pope John Paul II promulgated the new Code of Canon Law for the Latin Church. With the apostolic constitution *Sacrae disciplinae leges* ('Laws of sacred discipline'), the work of renewing the ecclesiastical order announced in 1959 by Pope John XXIII, simultaneously with the announcement of the Second Vatican Council, was completed. The new formulation of the Canon Law would become effective on November 27, 1983.

Upon the publication of the new Canon Law, it was immediately noticed that the word 'excommunication' no longer appeared in the new text, elating the Masonic organizations. Various Masonic institutions began informing their members that excommunication had been lifted, and brothers could attend church and receive the Eucharist.

Then came the cold shower. The day before the new C.I.C. came into effect, on November 26, 1983, the

Congregation for the Doctrine of the Faith, then led by Prefect Josef Ratzinger, provided the authentic interpretation of the code. Concerning Freemasonry, excommunication was still in force; it was imposed, without distinction, on all Masonic organizations, regardless of their greater or lesser anticlerical activities (excommunication *latae sententiae*).

Even though not all international Masonic lodges were equally anticatholic, the Catholic Church decided not to make any distinctions. The consequence of this clarification was that all those who professed to be Catholics and, despite that, frequented Masonic lodges were automatically excluded from the sacrament of the Eucharist due to their behaviour.

Those who continued to receive the Eucharist would have incurred a 'mortal sin,' meaning a state of grave moral responsibility. In the event that a person dies in this condition, their soul would go to hell. The use of the term 'mortal sin' indicates how this act leads to a rupture with God's saving grace. The soul, therefore, not only becomes weaker but dies.

One might wonder: why such severity from the Church towards Freemasonry? Just a few years after the establishment of speculative Freemasonry, the Holy See realized that, unlike operative Freemasonry, it was developing a program of activities clearly anticatholic and openly hostile to the papacy. The situation did not change in the following years, and the tension increased significantly, especially during the 'Risorgimento' period.

The Catholic Church was convinced that one of the objectives of Freemasonry was to instill such disgust for religion in the population as to lead to the loss of a significant portion of the faithful.

> Rome is not only the capital of Italy but also of Freemasonry: Albert Pike had predicted it, designating it as the second seat of the *Palladian Rite*[153] even before appointing Adriano Lemmi as his successor in the global leadership of the Supreme Councils of the 33°. In 1894, Lemmi was invested, and the leadership of the Palladian Rite landed in Rome. The process of destroying the papal spiritual power seemed imminent and irreversible: abuses and aggressions, thefts and humiliations against Catholics constituted for years the norm in liberated territories, with the total indifference of European powers claiming to be Catholic[154].

---

[153] «We must let all the (Masonic) Federations continue as they are, with their systems, their central authorities, and their various methods of correspondence among the higher degrees of the same rite, organized as they currently are. Instead, we must create a Supreme Rite, which will remain secret, in which we will convene those high-degree Masons that we choose. Toward the other brothers in Masonry, we must demand the utmost secrecy. Through this Supreme Rite, we will govern over Masonry, which will thus become an even more powerful international center because its direction will be unknown». From a letter sent by Mazzini to Pike on January 22, 1870. In: Edith Starr Millar (Lady Queenborough), (2009), Occult Theocrazy, Scotts Valley, Cal. USA, CreateSpace.

[154] Epiphanius, *Massoneria e sette segrete. (wk. cited).* p. 192.

To describe the atmosphere prevailing in the Italian peninsula shortly after the unification of Italy, a quote from a writing by Adriano Lemmi might suffice. The Grand Master of the G.·.O.·.I.·. and the leader of the super-Masonry that was the Palladian Rite published an article in 1886 in the Masonic Review, revealing the Italian Freemasonry's determination to stop at all costs 'the most fierce, stubborn, and ferocious enemy: the papacy[155].'

The Hero of the Two Worlds (Giuseppe Garibaldi) was no less explicit. Here is how he defined Pope Pius IX: 'a cubic meter of manure'... and further: «the most harmful of all creatures because he, more than anyone else, is an obstacle to human progress, to the brotherhood of men and peoples[156]»... «If a society of demons were to arise, fighting despotism and priests, I would enlist in its ranks[157]».

In those years, the political leaders at the helm of united Italy were named Depretis, Cairoli, Lanza, Zanardelli, Crispi, Di Rudini. Straddling the 19th and 20th centuries, the common element among all these prominent figures in Italian political life was their membership in Freemasonry and the desire to give a

---

[155] Corecco E., conference: *La Chiesa e la Massoneria. (wk. cited).* p. 2.
[156] Garibaldi G., 1907, *Scritti politici e militari. Ricordi e pensieri inediti.* Roma, Italia, E. Voghera, p. 823-24.
[157] *Ivi,* p. 829.

blow to the Christian tradition. Due to constant anticlerical propaganda and incessant defamation of the Catholic Church and the papacy, it became inevitable for the Holy See to stiffen and completely close itself off from any form of Masonic association.

These were the circumstances leading to the formulation of Canon 2335 of the 1917 C.I.C. (Code of Canon Law).

What kind of Relationship is possible between Chivalry and Freemasonry?

To fully answer this question, it is necessary to define what is meant by the term 'relationship.' Entering into a relationship is an act that seeks to verify whether there are points of contact, analogies, convergences, shared values, and not dissimilar purposes between two subjects, in this case, between the two institutions - Chivalry and Freemasonry. From the reading of the documents published as attachments, it clearly emerges that the Church of Rome does not allow Christians to belong to the spiritual Chivalry and Freemasonry simultaneously. This is because adherence to Freemasonry calls into question the foundations of being a Christian. Indeed, for the Christian, every other Christian, wherever they are born, regardless of their status, education, and residence, is a brother. On the other hand, the Freemason considers a brother only someone who has been initiated into Freemasonry and is an active member of a regular lodge.

As evident from the reading of the Declaration of the German Episcopal Conference (pp. 193-208), Freemasonry frequently resorts to sacredness (ritual opening of proceedings, opening of the book of the Sacred Law), which seems to mimic the religiosity and ritualism that have always been characteristic of Christianity.

In the same way that in the Eucharist, bread and wine transform (transubstantiation) into the body and blood of Christ, a transformation also occurs in the Masonic temple. In this case, it is man who undergoes the transformation. The initial condition is symbolically represented by the rough stone (the neophyte); this stone, through a joint effort by the adept and the institution, will be carved, polished, and shaped into a cubic stone (the Masonic Master). This 'New Man,' reborn at the end of a long initiatory journey, will be the cornerstone of a new humanity.

Another aspect that prevents the Catholic Church from having a relationship with Freemasonry is that in Masonic rituals, there is no reference to the figure of Jesus Christ or His Church. This attitude is because, for the Mason, Christianity is just one of the many forms through which man approaches the spiritual world. For Freemasonry, Hinduism, Buddhism, shamanism, Islam, polytheism, etc., are equivalent ways of relating to the Supreme Being.

A Catholic entering Freemasonry, if he truly understands the meaning of the phrases uttered during the initiation ritual and comprehends the sense and purposes of Masonic thought on religion, must be aware that, at the precise moment he enters a Masonic lodge, he is renouncing his faith in the Trinitarian God. For a Catholic, this act, done consciously, is considered a serious sin from a spiritual standpoint, as it is not only committed against God but also against all the brethren and sisters united by the same faith in Jesus Christ.

Ramon Llull clearly outlined the characteristics of a squire aspiring to become a spiritual Knight, that is, a Knight of Christ. In the fourth chapter of the *Llibre de l'Orde de Cavalleria* (wk.cit., p. 119), he recalls that on the day of investiture, the neosquire must deliver a sermon in which the fourteen articles forming the basis of faith in Christ, the Ten Commandments, the seven sacraments of the Holy Church, and other matters pertaining to faith are recounted. The neosquire must remember all these things well to reconcile the duties of chivalry with matters belonging to the Catholic faith. Let's examine them in detail:

> [5] The fourteen articles are as follows: believing in God is the first article. Believing in the Father, the Son, and the Holy Spirit constitutes three articles; one must believe that the Father, the Son, and the Holy Spirit are an eternal God, without end or beginning. Believing that God is the creator of everything that exists is the fifth. The sixth is believing that God is the redeemer, the one who redeemed humanity from the sins of Adam and Eve. The seventh is believing that God will glorify all those who are in paradise. These seven articles belong to the divine. The next seven belong to humanity that the Son of God took upon himself through our Lady Saint Mary; these are the seven articles: Believing that Jesus Christ was conceived by the Holy Spirit when Archangel Gabriel greeted Our Lady is the first. The second is

believing that Jesus Christ was born. The third is believing that he was crucified and killed for our salvation. The fourth is that his soul descended to hell to free Adam, Abraham, and the rest of the prophets who believed in his coming before their death. The fifth is believing that Jesus Christ rose. The sixth is believing that he ascended to heaven on the day of Ascension. The seventh is believing that Jesus Christ will return on the day of judgment when all of us will be resurrected, and he will judge the good and the bad. All men are obligated to believe in these fourteen articles, which testify to God and His works; no one can be saved without these articles.

[6] The Ten Commandments that God gave to Moses on Mount Sinai are as follows: You shall serve and worship only one God. Do not take the Lord's name in vain. Keep the Sabbath day holy. Honor your father and mother. Do not commit murder. Do not commit adultery. Do not steal. Do not bear false witness. Do not covet your neighbour's wife. Do not covet your neighbour's goods. All knights must be aware of these Ten Commandments so that the order does not violate the commandments given by God.

[7] The seven sacraments of the Holy Church are as follows: baptism, confirmation, the

> sacrifice of the altar, penance for one's sins, the sacraments administered by the bishop when consecrating a priest, a deacon, and a subdeacon, marriage, and the anointing. These are the seven sacraments through which we must be saved. The sacrament of chivalry must honour and fulfil these seven sacraments; therefore, all knights must know the duties of their office.

A knight must be aware that, should he decide to receive Masonic initiation, this event would automatically acquire the status of excommunication *latae sententiae*. In other words, he could no longer receive the sacrament of the Eucharist. Members of the knighthood order cannot adhere to Buddhist, Islamic, or Shinto beliefs, nor can they be devoted to the Great Architect of the Universe, as their calling, role, and continued membership in the order are closely tied to faith in Christ and the defence of Christianity.

The Templar knighthood was a product of the medieval Christian faith; the knights with white mantles are remembered to this day for being warriors willing to die for Christ. They have never considered pagans or Muslims as their brothers since they belong to forces operating against Christianity. The knight has faith in the God of Catholics, a God who intervenes in history, gives man the tablets of the law, moral norms, and sent His only son to redeem humanity from original sin. His creed is that Jesus Christ died on the cross and rose on the third day.

The knight, being a soldier of Christ, can never align himself with the Masonic vision of the G.·.A.·.D.·.U.·.. The Great Architect of the Universe in Masonry is a completely different entity from the God of Catholics. He does not intervene in human history, has no sons to send to Earth, does not judge, does not give rewards or punishments. The G.·.A.·.D.·.U.·. is an ideal, a concept, a container to be interpreted and filled with meanings, as Masonry, not being a religion, lacks its own theology and even its own god. The G.·.A.·.D.·.U.·. is a universal principle that unites all faiths and can be well expressed by reason.

Unlike the Christian knight, the Freemason rejects any revealed truth, any dogma, and places no limits on the search for truth. Rational thinking and past experiences guide man in what is permissible and what is not. Members of the spiritual knighthood are aware that one cannot simultaneously fight under two banners as distant and different as faith in Christ and Freemasonry. A true knight, worthy of the name, will never abandon his order to join an institution like Freemasonry that would deprive him of the joy of participating in the Eucharist.

While there may be Masons who disguise themselves under the white robes of chivalry or knights who, failing their oath, attend lodges, these are individual and unwise choices, on which there is little to add. The fact that chivalry, being inherently Christian, cannot have a relationship with Freemasonry due to its positions openly conflicting with the Catholic Church does not mean that there cannot be dialogues.

Meetings between the German Episcopate and German lodges in the recent past are an example. Moments of dialogue and reflection with representatives of Freemasonry would be appropriate to clearly explain the position of the Catholic Church to those knights who wear the square and compass around their necks instead of the crucifix and who may be convinced that there is nothing wrong with their choices.

From this situation, there should arise a reflection. Why do a certain number of Masons want to enter the order of chivalry? Why are a certain number of knights attracted to Freemasonry? Although the chivalric orders that originated within Freemasonry, the so-called 'high degrees' part of the Scottish Rite, are not the true chivalry (in the sense praised by Bernard de Clairvaux and revisited by Ramon Llull), an analysis of this phenomenon, this double flow, would certainly be appropriate.

Regarding the reasons that drive a certain number of members of the spiritual knighthood and ordinary Christ believers to cross the columns of Masonic temples, we cannot exclude that they fall within a misguided yearning for freedom, an obsessive search for mystery and the occult.

It is evident to everyone that lately, during religious functions, the majority of attendees are people with white hair. What are the reasons for the reduction in the number of believers? What are the reasons for the closure of many seminaries? Is the aggressive action of Freemasonry perhaps the cause of this crisis? I would say no, especially because the themes most debated in contemporary society today exactly echo the Masonic view of reality. Secularism, the desire for decision-making and moral autonomy, anti-dogmatism, emancipation, breaking the chains of uniform thinking, individual freedoms, fluid thinking, *political correctness*, and *new-age* thinking are its cornerstones.

In the eyes of Freemasonry, the Catholic world today represents the rearguard, stale confessionalism, a clan of sexists fixated on patriarchal family models. The themes and values promoted by Freemasonry have now emerged from the lodges and are spreading throughout society.

As a result, Catholic positions on abortion, euthanasia, same-sex unions, surrogacy, rejection of contraceptive use, and the right to assisted suicide are considered entirely outdated. Let's now look at the problem from another angle. Is it possible that the lack of interest in spirituality and religion that we observe today is somehow related to a boring, repetitive, and outdated catechesis by a certain clergy that is stressed, exhausted, aging, and no longer up to its tasks?

As it is known, only the unwise are convinced that mistakes are exclusively the result of others' behaviour. With this reflection in mind, it is natural to wonder if the Holy See should take new measures.

Regarding the relationship between Chivalry and Freemasonry, the Holy See's practice of maintaining established relations exclusively with recognized chivalric orders, while distancing itself from chivalric groups with proven Catholic faith, albeit few in number, might be a factor that has led Freemasonry to welcome them. The same has occurred with autocephalous Orthodox churches, which have welcomed chivalric groups of various origins into their functions.

Given the Catholic Church's longstanding openness to dialogue, what is surprising is the lack of communication with various chivalric groups operating in Italy. It is worth considering whether it would be appropriate for the Catholic Church to analyse the 'chivalry' issue in its complexity and multifaceted composition. It would certainly not be useless to conduct a census of these organizations to assess whether they represent mere chaff or if there is also some wheat.

Perhaps the various chivalric groups currently operating in Italy deserve careful evaluation regarding their goals, methods of operation, and individual characteristics. Why not offer spiritual guidance to groups that may request it? The presence of a chaplain could be a valuable aid to these groups and a useful tool to shed light on this sector, where misinformation is prevalent.

To serve in a chivalric group rooted in Christian tradition is not synonymous with bigotry or beguinage. Being a knight does not imply being reactionary or antimodern. Belonging to chivalry signifies a willingness to make oneself available to fight for the defence of principles that have always formed the foundations of the Christian tradition.

Chivalry has been dedicated to defending the Holy Land, the Holy Sepulcher, sacred Christian sites, pilgrims, and the clergy for centuries. Today, access to the sacred sites of Christianity in Palestine and other parts of the world is guaranteed. Therefore, terms like 'battle,' 'combat,' and 'struggle' should be understood as a strong commitment of chivalry to vigilantly ensure that Christians can worship their God anywhere in the world. Wearing a sword at the waist no longer holds a military significance but serves as a testimony to a challenging and tumultuous past.

In recent times, new objectives have emerged: the defence of the individual's dignity from conception to natural death; the protection of vulnerable individuals; the defence of marriage understood as a monogamous relationship between a man and a woman; and the defence of the right to religious freedom[158].

Being a knight today does not solely entail looking to the past, the Crusades, Palestine, physical strength, combat, or military skills. The gaze of the Knight of Christ is, with great attention, directed towards society's present and future.

---

[158] Doctrinal Note on Some Questions Regarding the Participation of Catholics in Political Life, pp. 225-244.

What was admirably expressed by Ramon Llull in the 13th century remains entirely relevant. The order of Chivalry must shape individuals capable of being moral guides for society. From these brief reflections, it is clear that there are no analogies, convergences, or common paths between the Catholic Church and Freemasonry.

While acknowledging that these two positions are irreconcilable, spiritual chivalry should not exclude the possibility of building moments of collaboration even with those chivalric associations expressing Masonic thought. However, it must be clear that this can only happen based on cultural, social, and bioethical projects and solidarity aimed at serving humanity and protecting human rights.

Charges of a Freemason

Extracted from the ancient Records of Lodges beyond Sea, and of those in England, Scotland, and Ireland, for the use of the Lodges in London: To be read at the making of New Brethren, or when the Master shall order it.

The GENERAL HEDS, viz.

I. OF GOD AND RELIGION.

II. OF THE CIVIL MAGISTRATE SUPREME AND SUBORDINATE.

III. OF LODGES.

IV. OF MASTERS, WARDENS, FELLOWS, AND APPRENTICES.

V. OF THE MANAGEMENT OF THE CRAFT IN WORKING.

VI. OF BEHAVIOUR, viz.

- A. In the Lodge while constituted.
- B. After the Lodge is over and the Brethren not gone.
- C. When Brethren meet without Strangers, but not in a Lodge.
- D. In Presence of Strangers not Masons.
- E. At Home, and in the Neighbourhood.
- F. Towards a strange Brother.

I. Concerning God and Religion

A Mason is oblig'd by his tenure to obey the moral law, and if he rightly understands the Art, he will never be a stupid atheist, nor an irreligious libertine. But though in ancient times Masons were charg'd in every country to be of the religion of that country or nation, whatever it was, yet 'tis now thought more expedient only to oblige them to that religion in which all men agree, leaving their particular opinions to themselves; that is, to be good men and true, or men of honour and honesty, by whatever denominations or persuasions they may be distinguish'd; whereby Masonry becomes the center of union, and the means of conciliating true friendship among persons that must else have remain'd at a perpetual distance.

II. Of the Civil Magistrate Supreme and Subordinate

A Mason is a peaceable subject to the civil powers, wherever he resides or works, and is never to be concern'd in plots and conspiracies against the peace and welfare of the nation, nor to behave himself undutiful to inferior Magistrates; for as Masonry hath been always injured by war, bloodshed, and confusion, so ancient kings and princes have been much dispos'd to encourage the Craftsmen, because of their peaceableness and loyalty, whereby they practically answer'd the cavils of their adversaries and promoted the honour of the Fraternity, whoever flourish'd in times of peace. So that if a Brother should be a rebel against the state, he is not to be countenanc'd in his rebellion; however, he may be pitied as an unhappy man; and if convicted of no other crime, though the loyal Brotherhood must and ought to disown his rebellion, and give no umbrage or ground of political jealousy to the government for the time being; they cannot expel him from the Lodge, and his relation to it remains indefeasible.

III. Of Lodges

A Lodge is a place where Masons assemble and work; hence, that assembly, or duly organiz'd society of Masons, is call'd a Lodge, and every Brother ought to belong to one and to be subject to its By-Laws and the General Regulations. It is either particular or general, and will be best understood by attending it, and by the regulations of the General or Grand Lodge hereunto annex'd. In ancient times no Master or Fellow could be absent from it, especially when warn'd to appear at it, without incurring a severe censure, until it appears to the Master and Wardens, that pure necessity hinder'd him. The persons admitted members of a Lodge must be good and true men, free-born, and of mature and discreet age, no bondmen, no women, no immoral or scandalous men, but of good report.

IV. Of Masters, Wardens, Fellows, and Apprentices

All preferment among Masons is grounded upon real worth and personal merit only; that so the Lords may be well served, the Brethren not put to shame, nor the Royal Craft despis'd: Therefore no Master or Warden is chosen by seniority, but for his merit. It is impossible to describe these things in writing, and every Brother must attend in his place, and learn them in a way peculiar to this Fraternity: only candidates may know, that no Master should take an Apprentice, unless he has sufficient Employment for him, and unless he be a perfect Youth, having no maim or defect in his Body, that may render him uncapable of learning the Art, of serving his Master's Lord, and of being made a Brother, and then a Fellow Craft in due time, even after he has served such a term of years as the custom of the country directs; and that he should be descended of honest parents; that so, when otherwise qualify'd, he may arrive to the honour of being the Warden, and then the Master of the Lodge, the Grand Warden, and at length the Grand Master of all the Lodges, according to his merit. No Brother can be a Warden until he has pass'd the part of a Fellow Craft; nor a Master until he has acted as a Warden, nor Grand Warden until he has been Master of a Lodge, nor Grand Master unless he has been a Fellow Craft before his election, who is also to be nobly born, or a gentleman of the best fashion, or some eminent scholar, or some curious architect, or other artist, descended of honest parents, and who is of singular great merit in the opinion of the Lodges. And for the better, and easier, and more honourable discharge of his office, the Grand-Master has a power to chuse his own Deputy Grand Master, who must be then, or must have been formerly, the Master of a particular Lodge, and has the privilege of acting whatever the Grand Master, his Principal, should act, unless the said Principal be present, or interpose his authority by a letter. These rulers and governors, supreme and subordinate, of the ancient Lodge, are to be obey'd in their respective stations by all the Brethren, according to the old Charges and regulations, with all humility, reverence, love, and alacrity.

V. Of The Management Of The Craft In Working

All Masons shall work honestly on working days, that they may live creditably on holy days, and the time appointed by the law of the land, or confirm'd by custom, shall be observ'd. The most expert of the Fellow Craftsmen shall be chosen or appointed the Master, or overseer of the Lord's Work; who is to be call'd Master by those that work under him. The Craftsmen are to avoid all ill language, call each other by no disobliging name, but Brother or Fellow; and behave themselves courteously within and without the Lodge. The Master, knowing himself to be able of cunning, shall undertake the Lord's Work as reasonably as possible, and truly dispend his Goods as if they were his own, nor to give more wages to any Brother or Apprentice than he really may deserve. Both the Master and the Masons receiving their wages justly, shall be faithful to the Lord, and honestly finish their Work, whether task or journey. Nor put the work to task that hath been accustomed to Journey. None shall discover envy at the prosperity of a Brother, nor supplant him or put him out of his work, if he be capable to finish the same; for no Man can finish another's work so much to the Lord's profit, unless he be thoroughly acquainted with the design and draughts of him that began it. When a Fellow Craftsman is chosen Warden of the work under the Master, he shall be true both to Master and Fellows, shall carefully oversee the Work in the Master's absence to the Lord's profit; and his Brethren shall obey him. All Masons employ'd, shall meekly receive their wages without murmuring or mutiny, and not desert the Master till the Work is finish'd. A younger Brother shall be instructed in working, to prevent spoiling the materials for want of judgment, and for encreasing and continuing of Brotherly love. The Grand Lodge shall approve all the tools used in working. No labourer shall be employ'd in the proper work of Masonry; nor shall Free-Masons work with those that are not free, without an urgent necessity; nor shall they teach labourers and unaccepted Masons, as they should teach a Brother or Fellow.

VI. Of Behaviour

A) *In the Lodge while constituted.*

You are not to hold private committees, or separate conversation, without leave from the Master, nor to talk of anything impertinent or unseemly, nor interrupt the Master or Wardens, or any Brother speaking to the Master: nor behave yourself ludicrously or jestingly while the Lodge is engaged in what is serious and solemn; nor use any unbecoming language upon any pretence whatsoever; but to pay due reverence to your Master, Wardens, and Fellows, and put them to worship.

If any complaint be brought, the Brother found guilty shall stand to the Award and determination of the Lodge, who are the proper and competent judges of all such controversies, (unless you carry it by appeal to the Grand Lodge) and to whom they ought to be referr'd, unless a Lord's work be hinder'd the meanwhile, in which case a particular reference may be made; but you must never go to law about what concerneth Masonry, without an absolute necessity apparent to the Lodge.

B) *Behaviour after the Lodge is over and the Brethren not gone.*

You may enjoy yourself with innocent mirth, treating one another according to ability, but avoiding all excess, or forcing any Brother to eat or drink beyond his Inclination, or hindering him from going when his occasions call him, or doing or saying anything offensive, or that may forbid an easy and free conversation for that would blast our harmony, and defeat our laudable purposes.

Therefore no private piques or quarrels must be brought within the door of the Lodge, far less any quarrels about religion, or nations, or state-policy, we being only, as Masons, of the Catholic religion above-mention'd; we are also of all nations, tongues, kindreds, and languages, and are resolv'd against alm politicks, as what never yet conduc'd to the welfare of the Lodge, nor ever will. This Charge has been always strictly enjoin'd and observ'd; but especially ever since the Reformation in Britain, or the dissent and secession of these nations from the communion of Rome.

C) *Behaviour when Brethren meet without strangers, but not in a Lodge form'd.*

You are to salute one another in a courteous manner, as you will be instructed, calling each other Brother, freely giving mutual Instruction as shall be thought expedient, without being overseen or overheard, and without encroaching upon each other, or derogating from that respect which is due to any Brother, were he not a Mason: For though all Masons are as Brethren upon the same Level, yet Masonry takes no Honour from a Man that he had before; nay rather it adds to his Honour, especially if he has deserv'd well of the Brotherhood, who must give Honour to whom it is due, and avoid ill manners.

D) *Behaviour in the presence of strangers not Masons.*

You shall be cautious in your words and carriage that the most penetrating stranger shall not be able to discover or find out what is not proper to be intimated, and sometimes you shall divert a discourse, and manage it prudently for the honour of the worshipful Fraternity.

E) *Behaviour at home, and in your neighbourhood.*

You are to act as becomes a moral and wise man; particularly, not to let your family, friends, and neighbours know the concerns of the Lodge, etc., but wisely to consult your own honour, and that of the ancient Brotherhood, for reasons not to be mention'd here. You must also consult your Health, by not continuing together too late, or too long from home, after Lodge hours are past; and by avoiding of gluttony or drunkenness, that your families be not neglected or injured, nor you disabled from working.

F) *Behaviour towards a strange Brother.*

You are cautiously to examine him, in such a method as prudence shall direct you, that you may not be impos'd upon by an ignorant false Pretender, whom you are to reject with contempt and derision, and beware of giving him any Hints of Knowledge.

But if you discover him to be a true and genuine Brother, you are to respect him accordingly; and if he is in want, you must relieve him if you can, or else direct him how he may be reliev'd: You must employ him some days, or else recommend him to be employ'd.

But you are not charged to do beyond your ability, only to prefer a poor Brother, who is a good man and true, before any other poor people in the same circumstances.

Finally, all these Charges you are to observe, and also those that shall be communicated to you in another way; cultivating brotherly love, the foundation and cape-stone, the cement and glory of this ancient fraternity, avoiding all wrangling and quarrelling, all slander and backbiting, nor permitting others to slander any honest brother, but defending his character, and doing him all good offices, as far as is consistent with your honour and safety, and no farther.

And if any of them do you Injury, you must apply to your own or his Lodge and from thence you may appeal to the Grand Lodge at the quarterly communication, and from thence to the annual Grand Lodge, as has been the ancient laudable conduct of our fore-fathers in every nation; never taking a legal course but when the case cannot be otherwise decided, and patiently listening to the honest and friendly advice of Master and Fellows, when they would prevent your going to law with strangers, or would excite you to put a speedy period to all law-suits, that so you may mind the affair of Masonry with the more alacrity and success; but with respect to Brothers or Fellows at law, the Master and Brethren should kindly offer their mediation, which ought to be thankfully submitted to by the contending Brethren; and if that submission is impracticable, they must however carry on their process or law-suit without wrath and rancor (not in the common way) saying or doing nothing which may hinder brotherly-love, and good Offices to be renew'd and continu'd; that all may see the benign Influence of Masonry, as all true Masons have done from the beginning of the world, and will do to the end of time.

Amen, so mote it be.

In Eminenti Apostolatus Specula[159]

CLEMENT[160], BISHOP, Servant of the Servants of God to all the faithful, Salutation, and Apostolic Benediction.

Since the divine clemency has placed Us, Whose merits are not equal to the task, in the high watch-tower of the Apostolate with the duty of pastoral care confided to Us, We have turned Our attention, as far as it has been granted Us from on high, with unceasing care to those things through which the integrity of Orthodox Religion is kept from errors and vices by preventing their entry, and by which the dangers of disturbance in the most troubled times are repelled from the whole Catholic World.

Now it has come to Our ears, and common gossip has made clear, that certain Societies, Companies, Assemblies, Meetings, Congregations or Conventicles called in the popular tongue Free Masons or *Francs Maçons* or by other names according to the various languages, are spreading far and wide and daily growing in strength; and men of any Religion or sect, satisfied with the appearance of natural probity, are joined

---

[159] *In eminenti apostolatus specula* is a Papal Bull dealing with the condemnation of Freemasonry, issued in 1738. *In eminenti apostolatus specula,* issued in 1738, translates to "In the eminet seat of the apostolate".

[160] Pope Clement XII, born as Lorenzo Corsini (1652-1740), served as the 246th pope of the Catholic Church from 1730 to 1740.

together, according to their laws and the statutes laid down for them, by a strict and unbreakable bond which obliges them, both by an oath upon the Holy Bible and by a host of grievous punishment, to an inviolable silence about all that they do in secret together.

But, given the nature of the offense to manifest itself and generate the noise that denounces it, it follows that the aforementioned societies or convents have generated such suspicion in the minds of the faithful. According to this suspicion, for honest and prudent individuals, joining these associations is tantamount to staining oneself with the infamy of wickedness and perversion. If they did not act unjustly, they would not vehemently hate the light. This reputation has grown so considerably that these societies have already been proscribed by secular princes in many countries as enemies of the realms and have been prudently eliminated.

Therefore, contemplating the most serious harm that such societies or clandestine assemblies often cause not only to the tranquillity of the temporal republic but also to the spiritual health of souls, as they do not align in any way with either Civil Laws or Canonical Laws, and instructed by the Divine words to watch day and night like a faithful and prudent servant appointed to the household of the Lord, so that this kind of people may not plunder the house like thieves or ruin the vineyard like foxes, i.e., corrupting the hearts of the simple and secretly harming the innocent, and aiming to close the path that, if left open, might allow crimes with impunity, for other just and rational reasons known to us, with the advice of some of our venerable Cardinal Brothers of the Holy Roman Church, and also of our own accord (*motu proprio*), with secure knowledge, mature deliberation, and the fullness of our apostolic authority, we decree that it should be condemned and prohibited. By means of this, Our Constitution, valid in perpetuity, we condemn and prohibit the aforementioned societies, unions, gatherings, assemblies, associations, or clandestine assemblies of *Free Masons* or *Francs Maçons*, or by any other name they may be called.

Wherefore, We command most strictly and in virtue of holy obedience, all the faithful of whatever state, grade, condition, order, dignity or pre-eminence, whether clerical or lay, secular or regular, even those who are entitled to specific and individual mention, that none, under any pretext or for any reason, shall dare or presume to enter, propagate or support these aforesaid societies of *Free Masons* or *Francs Maçons*, or however else they are called, or to receive them in their houses or dwellings or to hide them, be enrolled among them, joined to them, be present with them, give power or permission for them to meet elsewhere, to help them in any way, to give them in any way advice, encouragement or support either openly or in secret, directly or indirectly, on their own or through others; nor are they to urge others or tell them, incite or persuade them to be enrolled in such societies or to be counted among their number, or to be present or to assist them in any way; but they must stay completely clear of such Societies, Companies, Assemblies, Meetings, Congregations or Conventicles, under pain of excommunication for all the above mentioned people, which is incurred *ipso facto* (by the very deed) without any declaration being required, and from which no one can obtain the benefit of absolution, other than at the hour of death, except through Ourselves or the Roman Pontiff *pro tempore* (of the time).

Moreover, We desire and command that both Bishops and prelates, and other local ordinaries, as well as inquisitors for heresy, shall investigate and proceed against transgressors of whatever state, grade, condition, order dignity or pre-eminence they may be; and they are to pursue and punish them with condign penalties as being most suspect of heresy.

Consequently, we grant and give them, and each of them, the free authority to proceed and inquire against the aforementioned transgressors, to imprison them, and to punish them with due penalties, also invoking, if necessary, the assistance of the secular arm.

We also wish that copies of this, even if printed, undersigned by the hand of some public notary and sealed by a person holding a position in Ecclesiastical dignity, be given the same faith as would be given to the letter if it were exhibited or shown in the original.

Therefore, let it be absolutely forbidden for anyone to violate or, with rash audacity, contradict this page of Our declaration, condemnation, command, prohibition, and interdiction. If anyone should dare to do so, let them know that they will incur the wrath of Almighty God and the Holy Apostles Peter and Paul.

Given at Rome, at Saint Mary Mayor, in the year 1738 of Our Lord.

Declaration of the Principles Approved by the Supreme Councils Held in Lausanne in September 1875

Freemasonry proclaims, as it has proclaimed since its origin, the existence of a creative Principle, under the name of the Grand Architect of the Universe.

It imposes no limits on the search for truth, and it is to guarantee this freedom to all that it demands tolerance from everyone.

Freemasonry is, therefore, open to men of all nationalities, races, and beliefs.

It prohibits political and religious discussions in its workshops, welcoming any profane individual regardless of their political and religious opinions, which it does not concern itself with, as long as they are free and of good moral character.

The purpose of Freemasonry is to combat ignorance in all its forms; it is a mutual school whose program can be summarized as follows: obey the laws of one's country, live honourably, practice justice, love one's neighbour, work tirelessly for the happiness of humanity, and pursue its progressive and peaceful emancipation.

That is what Freemasonry adopts and seeks to have adopted by those who desire to belong to the Masonic family.

But alongside this declaration of principles, the Convention needs to proclaim the doctrines on which Masonry is based; it wants everyone to know them.

To uplift man in his own eyes, to make him worthy of his mission on earth, Masonry posits as a principle that the Supreme Creator has given man, as his most precious possession, freedom; freedom, the heritage of all humanity, a ray from above that no power has the right to extinguish or dampen and which is the source of feelings of honour and dignity.

From the preparation for the first degree to the attainment of the highest degree of Scottish Masonry, the first condition without which nothing is granted to the aspirant is an undisputed reputation for honour and probity.

To those for whom religion is the supreme consolation, Masonry says: «Cultivate your religion without hindrance, follow the inspirations of your conscience». Freemasonry is not a religion, it does not have a cult; hence, it advocates secular education, and its doctrine is entirely encapsulated in this beautiful injunction: «Love thy neighbour».

To those who rightfully fear political discord, Masonry says: «I proscribe all political discussion, all political debate from my meetings; be a faithful and devoted servant to your country, you have no account to render to us. The love of the country aligns so well with the practice of all virtues!»

Masonry has been accused of immorality! Our morality is the purest, the holiest; it is based on the first of all virtues: humanity. The true Mason does good, and extends his care to the unfortunate, whoever they may be, to the extent of his own situation. Therefore, he can only reject immorality with disgust and contempt.

These are the foundations on which Freemasonry rests, ensuring the closest union for all members of this great family; regardless of the distance separating the various countries they inhabit, love is the bond among them all. And who can better attest to this truth than the very assembly of our Convention?

Unknown to each other, coming from the most diverse countries, we had barely exchanged the first words of welcome, and already the closest union prevailed among us; hands were shaking fraternally, and it is within the most touching harmony that our most important resolutions were unanimously adopted.

Freemasons from all corners, citizens of all countries, these are the precepts, these are the laws of Freemasonry, these are its mysteries. Against it, the efforts of calumny remain powerless, and its insults will remain without an echo; peacefully advancing from victory to victory, Freemasonry will extend its moral and civilizing influence every day.

Declaration of the German Episcopal Conference on Catholic Membership in Freemasonry[161]

Towards the end of the eighth decade of the 20th century, there was much discussion and speculation about the 'abrogation of excommunication' and the 'Reconciliation between the Church and Freemasonry.' However, during that period, the episcopate of the Federal Republic of Germany released a document expressing a different opinion.

Expositions of the Discussions between Representatives of the Catholic Church and Freemasonry:

I. Starting Point

1. *The talks*

In the years 1974-1980, official talks were conducted in Germany between representatives of the German Episcopal Conference and the United Grand Lodges of Germany on behalf of the Catholic Church and Freemasonry.

2. *The mandate*

The German Episcopal Conference had tasked the dialogue group with the following mandates:

[161] Alleanza Cattolica - Cristianità n. 66 (1980) - October 29, 1980.

a) Assessment of changes within Freemasonry in Germany;
b) Examination of the compatibility of simultaneous membership in the Catholic Church and Freemasonry;
c) In the case of an affirmative answer to the previous question, public preparation of public opinion for the changed situation.

3. *The situation among Masons*

German Freemasonry emerged from National Socialist persecution significantly reduced, comprising about a quarter of its previous size. This reduction may have contributed to changes, fostering a certain openness towards other social groups. Based on this situation, the interest of Freemasonry in clarifying its relationship with Christian Churches has also emerged.

4. *Vatican II and the Encyclical 'Ecclesiam Suam'*

In the Second Vatican Council, the Church opened itself to dialogue with all people 'of good will,' engaging in conversations with any group willing to participate.

This intention, documented in various conciliar texts, was further developed by Pope Paul VI in his programmatic encyclical 'Ecclesiam Suam,' which establishes its theoretical foundations more extensively and outlines practical guidelines. Above all, he identified different circles with which dialogue should be initiated, starting from one's own community to those who do not believe in God. Already during the Council, and increasingly after it, the necessity of dialogue with Freemasonry was recognized.

II. A Changed Image

1. *Humanitarian Concern*

The properly understood freedom of individuals in private, religious, and public life, as explicitly emphasized by the Church in Vatican II, served as a foundation for dialogue with Freemasonry. Freemasonry, in its humanitarian stance sees itself as obligated to advocate for human freedom. This commitment extends analogously to the promotion of human rights.

2. *Charity*

German Freemasonry actively supports institutions dedicated to brotherly assistance and charity. It engages in relief initiatives for those in distress. Given that benevolence and charitable activities are integral to the mission of the Church, certain points of connection were also identified in this regard.

3. *Understanding of Symbols*

In our time, which is often characterized as disenchanted, many individuals look to the symbols and rituals of Freemasonry for a sense of fulfillment of otherwise unmet needs. In the Catholic Church, symbols and rituals have consistently held their significance. It is, therefore, assumed that there is a potential point of connection and a foundation for understanding in this context.

4. *Individual Masonic Personalities*

The integrity, qualifications, attitude, and personal opinions of specific Masonic individuals, who have stood out on various occasions, both within and outside ecclesiastical circles, have also played a role in fostering a positive disposition towards the Lodge.

5. *Common Commitment against Materialism*

Freemasonry has demonstrated its willingness on multiple occasions to engage in the fight against materialistic ideology and its dehumanizing consequences, often collaborating with Christian Churches.

6. *A New Relationship?*

Especially the factors highlighted in the preceding points 1-5 led to the belief that Freemasonry had undergone such a transformation that the Church's previous stance was surpassed. It was thought that any Catholic could now belong to a Masonic lodge without encountering issues.

7. *Action on Public Opinion*

The aforementioned perception of an apparent compatibility between membership in the Catholic Church and Freemasonry was disseminated through extensive efforts targeting public opinion. This included conferences, open lodge sessions, the publication of books, articles in newspapers, and magazines.

8. *The Copernican Revolution*

The mentioned perspective was supported by a specific and entirely erroneous interpretation of the last Council, which became apparent after the publicity campaigns. According to this interpretation, the Council, in a true Copernican revolution was believed to have cast aside the guiding idea of objective truth in the Church, replacing it with the concept of human dignity. This would result in a close relationship between the Catholic Church and Freemasonry.

III. The Reaction of the Church

1. *Examination Procedure*

All the previously mentioned initiatives proved inadequate for a truly objective treatment of the problem and for reaching a well-founded and robust response. In this context, the integrity, opinion, and attitude of individual Masons are not determinative, as they are entirely subjective.

To conduct a genuinely objective examination of the problem, it was imperative to delve into the essence of Freemasonry as represented by the United Grand Lodges of Germany. Irrespective of any subjective views, the objective essence is revealed in the official rituals of Freemasonry. Consequently, these documents underwent a meticulous and prolonged examination (from 1974 to 1980). This scrutiny encompassed the rituals of the initial three degrees, with Masons permitting the study of the texts, although the discussions extended beyond the rituals alone.

2. *The Unchanged Position of Freemasonry*

The fact that Freemasonry fundamentally questions the Church has not changed. This circumstance becomes particularly clear when considering what self-understanding in concrete terms, ideal basis, present conception, and future perspective the Masons have given themselves as an animated and militant program in the document 'Theses for the year 2000,' published immediately after the conclusion of the talks.

In it, the objective value of revealed truth is denied in principle, and with this indifference, a revealed religion is excluded from the beginning. Already the first thesis, undoubtedly the most important, states: *«There are no systems of a philosophical-religious nature* (weltanschaulich-religiöser Art) *that can claim exclusive obligatoriness».*

3. *Improvements in Atmosphere. Practical Collaboration*

Compared to past centuries, the tone, manner, and level of expressing differences have improved and changed. If there were hostilities and insults before, today the discussion has risen to a level of objectivity. It is also important to note that the discussions took place in a serene atmosphere of openness and objectivity. It was possible to eliminate several untenable prejudices.

The Catholic Church now knows that it is obliged to collaborate with other religious communities and communities united by a specific worldview when it comes to achieving humanitarian and charitable goals. To the extent that similar goals are a priority for Masons, the Catholic Church is willing to engage in joint supportive action. However, it should not create the impression that the Church has reason to consider its attitude of caution and rejection towards Freemasonry as outdated.

4. *The Result of the Talks*

If the discussion on the first degree, already carried out previously by the Protestant Church, could not eliminate serious difficulties, the Catholic Church, in examining the first three degrees, had to acknowledge fundamental and insurmountable contrasts.

Freemasonry has not changed in its essence. Membership in it questions the foundations of Christian existence. The in-depth examination of the rituals of Freemasonry and the Masonic way of being, as well as its current unchanged self-understanding, make it clear *that contemporary membership in the Catholic Church and Freemasonry is excluded.*

The following are some of the objects and topics of discussion that led to this result. The commission also discussed others, no less important.

IV. Reasons for Incompatibility

1. *The vision that the Freemasons have of the world*

The Masonic perspective on the world is not rigidly defined. It is characterized by a humanitarian and ethical orientation. The rituals, comprising established texts with symbolic words and actions, offer a framework of representations that each individual Mason can interpret according to their personal beliefs. There is no presence of a universally binding ideology; rather, Masonic fundamental beliefs align with *relativism*.

The *International Masonic Lexicon*, acknowledged as an authoritative source, articulates: «Freemasonry is perhaps the sole institution that has managed to maintain, to a significant extent, freedom from dogmas in both ideology and practice».

Freemasonry can thus be understood a is a movement dedicated to uniting individuals with relativistic inclinations to advance the humanitarian ideal». This kind of subjectivism cannot be reconciled with the faith in the word of God, authentically revealed and interpreted by the Magisterium of the Church. Furthermore, It promotes a fundamental disposition that poses a threat to the Catholic approach to the words and actions within the sacramental and sacred life of the Church.

2. *The Masonic Concept of Truth*

Masons deny the possibility of objective knowledge of truth. During the talks, the well-known sentence by G. E. Lessing was mentioned: «If God were to hold all truth in His right hand and in His left hand the ever-living striving for truth, even with the addition that I always and eternally deceive myself, and He said to me, 'Choose,' I would humbly throw myself to His left and say, 'Father, give me! Pure truth is for You alone'».

The discussions pointed out that this view is characteristic of Freemasonry. The foundation of Freemasonry lies in the *relativity of every truth*. As Masons reject all faith in dogmas, they do not admit any dogma even within their lodges.

The Mason is therefore required to be a free man who «knows no submission to dogma and passion». This conditions the rejection, in principle, of all dogmatic positions, expressed in the Masonic Lexicon proposition: «All institutions based on dogma, the most eminent of which can be considered the Catholic Church, exert coercions on faith». Such a concept of truth is not compatible with the Catholic concept of truth, neither from the perspective of natural theology nor from that of the theology of revelation.

3. *The Masonic Concept of Religion*

The Masonic conception of religion is relativistic: all religions are competing attempts to express the divine truth, which ultimately is unattainable. To this divine truth, only the language of Masonic symbols, a language with many meanings, is adequate, left to the interpretative capacity of the individual Mason. Notably, the dispute on religious topics within the lodge is strictly forbidden to its members. In the Ancient Charges of 1732, at point I, it is stated: «The Mason, as a Mason, is bound to obey the moral law; if he understands the Art rightly, he will never be a bold denier of God, nor an unrestrained libertine. In ancient times, Masons were obliged in every country to belong to the religion in force in their country or people, but, today, it is considered more appropriate to obligate them only to the religion in which all men agree and leave each to his particular convictions». The concept of religion «in which all men agree» implies a relativistic view of religion, which cannot coincide with the fundamental conviction of Christianity.

4. *The Masonic Concept of God*

At the center of the rituals is the concept of the *Great Architect of the Universe.* Despite the goodwill to embrace every religion, it is a *deistic conception.* In this context, there is no objective knowledge of God in the sense of the personal concept of God in theism. The *Great Architect of the Universe* is a neutral, undefined 'It,' open to every possible understanding. Everyone can infuse their own conception of God into it, whether Christian, Muslim, Confucian, animist, or belonging to any religion.

The concept of the 'Architect of the Universe' within Freemasonry does not denote a personal God. Therefore, the acknowledgment of the 'Architect of the Universe' requires only a subjective and arbitrary sense of religious sentiment among its members. This depiction of a universal Architect reigning in a deistic distance undermines the foundations of the Catholic concept of God and their response to the God who addresses them as Father and Lord.

5. *The Masonic Concept of God and Revelation*

The Masonic conception of God does not permit consideration of a revelation of God, as is found in the faith and tradition of all Christians. Instead, with the concept of the *Great Architect of the Universe*, the relationship with God is returned to pre-deistic positions. Similarly, the explicit derivation of Christianity from the original astral religion of the Babylonians and Sumerians is in direct contradiction with the belief in Revelation.

6. *The Idea of Masonic Tolerance*

From this concept of truth, the idea of specific Masonic tolerance also arises. For Catholics, tolerance implies patient endurance owed to one's neighbour. Among Masons, however, there is tolerance towards ideas, no matter how opposing they may be. We refer again to Lennhoff-Posner: «From relativism, the Masonic position on the problems of man and humanity can be derived. [...] Relativism establishes tolerance with rational arguments.

Freemasonry is one of the movements that emerged at the end of the Middle Ages as a reaction against the absoluteness of the teaching of the Church and political absolutism, as a response to fanaticism of every kind». Such an idea of tolerance *shakes the Catholic's attitude of fidelity to his faith* and recognition of ecclesiastical authority.

7. R*itual Actions of Masons*

The three rituals of the apprentice, fellow, and master degrees have been discussed in extensive talks and explanations. These ritual actions manifest, in words and symbols, a character similar to that of the sacraments. They give the impression that, in such circumstances, objectively something is being done that transforms a person with symbolic actions. The content is a symbolic initiation of man that, in all its characteristics, competes with his sacramental transformation.

8. *The Perfection of Man*

According to what appears from the rituals, the ultimate goal of Freemasonry is to improve man to the highest degree from an ethical and spiritual perspective. In the rite of the master's degree, it is stated: «What virtues should a true master possess? Purity of heart, truth in words, prudence in actions, intrepidity in inevitable evils, and tireless zeal, if necessary, in doing good». In this regard, doubts could not be overcome that ethical perfection is absolutized, and so separated from grace that there is no longer any space for the justification of man according to the Christian conception. What purpose does the sacramental communication of salvation through baptism, penance, and the Eucharist serve when enlightenment and the triumph over death, as referenced in the fundamental three degrees, have already been accomplished?

9. *Masonic Spirituality*

Freemasonry presents itself to its members with a claim of totality that requires lifelong membership. Even if it is assumed that the path taken in the three degrees primarily pursues the goal of forming conscience and character, the problem remains whether the mission that the Church claims as its own allows for an institution alien to it to assume such a formative role. In this claim of totality, the incompatibility between Freemasonry and the Catholic Church becomes particularly evident.

10. *Different Currents within Freemasonry*

Within Freemasonry, in addition to the majority of lodges with a fundamentally humanitarian and 'belief in God' orientation, there are also extreme positions. On the one hand, there is the atheistic fraternity of the *Grand Orient de France*, which also has some lodges in Germany, and on the other hand, there is the *German Grosse Landesloge*, also known as the Christlicher Freimau Rerorden[162]. However, this 'Christian Masonry' is not outside the fundamental Masonic order; this term simply implies a broader possibility of reconciling Freemasonry with subjective Christian belief. Nevertheless, *it must be denied that this is achieved in a theologically satisfying way*, as the fundamental facts of the revelation of God become man and his communion with humanity are understood only as a possible variant of the Masonic worldview and are shared by only a small part of Masons.

11. *Freemasonry and the Catholic Church*

It is crucial to differentiate between Masonry that is well-disposed or neutral and Masonry that is hostile to the Church. However, in this context, the distinction can be misleading as it implies that, for Catholics, participation should only be excluded in cases of

---

[162] Christian Freemason Order

hostility to the Church. The examination has, in fact, extended to Masonry that is well-disposed towards the Catholic Church, and even in these instances, insurmountable difficulties had to be acknowledged.

12. *Masons and the Evangelical Church*

In 1973, discussions also took place at this level. The evangelical participants, in their concluding statement dated October 13, 1973, indeed «left it to the free assessment of the individual» regarding the possibility of dual membership. However, what is particularly noteworthy in this statement is highlighted in point 5: «It was not possible for the ecclesiastical participants in the talks to form a definitive idea about the ritual, concerning its meaning and the quality of the experience associated with it. They raised the question of whether the experience of the ritual and the work of the Mason could potentially diminish the significance that justification by grace holds for the evangelical Christian».

V. Concluding Declaration

Despite Freemasonry's transformation towards greater inclusivity following the persecution during the Nazi era, its mindset, core beliefs, and 'work in the temple' have remained entirely unaltered. The identified oppositions strike at the very foundations of Christian existence. Thorough investigations into Masonic rituals and the Masonic ideal world unequivocally establish that concurrent membership in the Catholic Church and Freemasonry is precluded.

Note: This final note in italics was prepared by the Secretariat of the German Episcopal Conference in response to the press release issued by the United Grand Lodges of Germany regarding the Declaration of the German Episcopal Conference.

1. *The Lichtenau Declaration of July 5, 1970, signed by three Catholics and nine Masons, did not receive any ecclesiastical authorization, either from a bishops' conference or from Roman authorities. Even Cardinal König, to whom the document was submitted, was unwilling to endorse it;*
2. *The reference to the Evangelical Church's declaration on Freemasonry is incomplete, as it is not mentioned that in the same declaration, it is also stated:* «It proved challenging for the ecclesiastical participants in the discussions to arrive at a conclusive understanding of the ritual, particularly concerning its meaning and the quality of the associated experience. In this context, they posed the question of whether the experience of the ritual and the practices of the Mason might compromise the significance that justification by grace holds for the evangelical Christian». *It's noteworthy that the Evangelical Church has only been able to scrutinize the first degree, and this examination took place with a*

scope and perspective distinct from that of the Catholic Church;

3. *The assertion that membership in Freemasonry challenges the fundamentals of Christian existence is not made in arrogance but arises from a meticulous exposition of the principles underlying Masonic self-perception.*

Declaration Regarding the Adherence of Catholics to Masonic Associations

Sacred Congregation for the Doctrine of the Faith

On July 19, 1974, the Sacred Congregation for the Doctrine of the Faith wrote a confidential letter to some Episcopal Conferences regarding the interpretation of Canon 2335 of the Code of Canon Law, which prohibits Catholics, under the penalty of excommunication, from joining Masonic associations and similar groups.

Since the aforementioned letter, which became public, has given rise to incorrect and biased interpretations, this Congregation, without prejudging the possible provisions of the new Code, confirms and specifies the following:

1. The current canonical discipline, which remains in full force, has not been modified in any way.
2. Therefore, excommunication and other prescribed penalties have not been abrogated.
3. What is referred to in the aforementioned letter regarding the interpretation of the canon in question should be understood, as was the intention of the Sacred Congregation, only as a reminder of the general principles of interpreting penal laws to resolve cases of individuals subject to the judgment of the Ordinaries.

It was not the intention of the Sacred Congregation to leave it to the Episcopal Conferences to publicly pronounce a general judgment on the nature of Masonic associations that implies derogations from the aforementioned norms.

Franjo Card. Šeper

Prefect

Fr. Jérôme Hamer, O.P., Titular Archbishop of Lorium

Secretary

Rome, from the Seat of the Sacred Congregation for the Doctrine of the Faith, on February 17, 1981.

Declaration on Freemasonry

Congregation for the Doctrine of the Faith.

The question has been raised whether the Church's judgment regarding Freemasonry has changed due to the fact that it is not expressly mentioned in the new Code of Canon Law as it was in the previous Code. This Congregation is able to respond that this circumstance is due to an editorial criterion followed for other associations as well, which are equally not mentioned because they fall under broader categories.

Therefore, the Church's negative judgment towards Masonic associations remains unchanged, as their principles have always been considered incompatible with the doctrine of the Church. Consequently, membership in them remains prohibited. The faithful who belong to Masonic associations are in a state of grave sin and cannot receive Eucharist. It is not within the competence of local ecclesiastical authorities to pronounce on the nature of Masonic associations with a judgment implying derogation from the above, in line with the Declaration of this Sacred Congregation on February 17, 1981 (Cf. AAS 73, 1981, p. 240-241).

His Holiness Pope John Paul II, during an audience granted to the undersigned Cardinal Prefect, has approved this Declaration, decided upon in the ordinary meeting of this Sacred Congregation, and has ordered its publication.

Joseph Card. Ratzinger
Prefect

Fr. Jérôme Hamer, O.P., Titular Archbishop of Lorium
Secretary

Rome, from the Seat of the Sacred Congregation for the Doctrine of the Faith, on November 26, 1983.

Reflections one year after the Declaration of the Congregation for the Doctrine of the Faith

Incompatibility between Christian Faith and Freemasonry

On November 26, 1983, the Congregation for the Doctrine of the Faith issued a declaration on Masonic associations. Just over a year after its publication, it may be useful to briefly illustrate the significance of this document[163].

Since the Church began to express its views on Freemasonry, its negative judgment has been inspired by multiple reasons, both practical and doctrinal. The Church has not only considered Masonry responsible for subversive activities against it, but from the earliest pontifical documents on the matter, particularly in the encyclical *Humanum Genus*[164] by Pope Leo XIII (April 20, 1884), the Magisterium of the Church denounced in Freemasonry philosophical ideas and moral concepts opposed to Catholic doctrine. For Leo XIII, these ideas essentially boiled down to rationalistic naturalism, inspiring its plans and activities against the Church.

---

[163] L'Osservatore Romano, February 23, 1985. (*wk. cited*).

[164] *Humanum Genus, (*'The Human Race'*)* is an Encylcic of Pope Leo XIII on Freemasonry, URL: *https://www.vatican.va/ content/ leo-xiii/en/encyclicals/documents/hf_lxiii_enc_18840420_huma num-genus.html* (*Verified 06-21-2023*).

In his Letter to the Italian People *Custodi*[165] (December 8, 1892), he wrote: «Let us remember that Christianity and Freemasonry are essentially incompatible, so that joining one means separating from the other». Therefore, it was essential to consider the positions of Freemasonry from a doctrinal perspective when, in the 1970s-1980s, the Sacred Congregation corresponded with some Episcopal Conferences particularly interested in this issue due to the dialogue undertaken by Catholic personalities with representatives of some lodges that declared themselves not hostile or even favourable to the Church.

Now, more in-depth study has led the Sacred Congregation for the Doctrine of the Faith to reaffirm its conviction of the fundamental incompatibility between the principles of Freemasonry and those of the Christian faith.

Therefore, regardless of the practical attitudes of different lodges, whether hostile or not towards the Church, the Sacred Congregation for the Doctrine of the Faith, in its declaration of November 26, 1983, aimed to address the deepest and essential level of the problem: the level of incompatibility of principles, which means on the level of faith and its moral requirements.

From this doctrinal standpoint, in continuity with the traditional position of the Church, as evidenced by

---

[165] *Custodi di Quella Fede*, ('Keepers of that Faith') in una Epistola di S.S. Leone XIII. URL: *https://www.vatican.va/content/leo-xiii/it/encyclicals/documents/hf_l-xiii_enc_08121892_custodi-di-quella-fede.html* (*Verified 09-30-2022*)

the aforementioned documents of Leo XIII, practical consequences then derive, applicable to all the faithful who might be members of Freemasonry.

Regarding the assertion of the incompatibility of principles, however, some argue that the essential nature of Freemasonry is precisely the fact that it does not impose any 'principle' in the sense of a philosophical or religious position binding for all its members. Instead, it gathers together, beyond the boundaries of different religions and worldviews, people of goodwill based on humanistic values understandable and acceptable to all.

Freemasonry would constitute a unifying element for all those who believe in the Architect of the Universe and feel committed to fundamental moral orientations defined, for example, in the Decalogue; it would not alienate anyone from their religion but, on the contrary, would serve as an incentive to adhere to it more strongly.

In this context, the numerous historical and philosophical issues underlying such claims cannot be discussed. That the Catholic Church also advocates for collaboration among all people of goodwill is certainly not necessary to emphasize after the Second Vatican Council. However, associating in Freemasonry decisively goes beyond this legitimate collaboration and has a meaning far more significant and determinative than this.

First of all, it must be remembered that the community of 'freemasons' and its moral obligations present themselves as a progressive system of symbols with an extremely engaging character. The rigid discipline of the arcane that dominates it further strengthens the weight of the interaction of signs and ideas. This climate of secrecy also entails the risk for members of becoming instruments of strategies unknown to them.

Even though it is asserted that relativism is not adopted as a dogma, it effectively proposes a relativistic symbolic conception. Therefore, the relativizing value of such a moral-ritual community, far from being eliminated, becomes decisive.

In this context, the various religious communities to which individual members of the Lodges belong can only be considered as simple institutionalizations of a broader and unattainable truth. The value of these institutionalizations appears inevitably relative to this broader truth, which manifests itself rather in the community of goodwill, that is, in the Masonic fraternity.

For a Catholic Christian, however, it is not possible to live his relationship with God in a dual manner, by splitting it into a humanitarian, non-denominational form and an internal, Christian form. He cannot cultivate relationships of two kinds with God, nor express his relationship with the Creator through symbolic forms of two kinds. This would be something completely different from the collaboration, which is evident to him, with all those who are committed to doing good, even if based on different principles.

Moreover, a Catholic Christian cannot at the same time participate in the full communion of the Christian fraternity and, on the other hand, look at his Christian brother, from the Masonic perspective, as a 'profane.'

Even when, as already mentioned, there is no explicit obligation to profess relativism as a doctrine, the relativizing force of such a fraternity, by its intrinsic logic, has the capacity to transform the structure of the act of faith so radically as to be unacceptable to a Christian, 'to whom his faith is dear' (Leo XIII).

This distortion in the fundamental structure of the act of faith occurs mostly in a subtle manner and without being noticed: the firm adherence to the truth of God, revealed in the Church, becomes a simple belonging to an institution, considered as a particular expressive form alongside other more or less equally possible and valid expressive forms of man's orientation to the eternal.

The temptation to go in this direction is now even stronger, as it fully corresponds to certain prevalent convictions in contemporary mentality. The opinion that truth cannot be known is a characteristic feature of our time and, at the same time, an essential element of its general crisis.

Starting from the consideration of all these elements, the Declaration of the Sacred Congregation asserts that membership in Masonic associations «remains prohibited by the Church», and the faithful who join them «are in a state of grave sin and cannot access Holy Communion».

With this final expression, the Sacred Congregation indicates to the faithful that such membership constitutes objectively a grave sin, and by specifying that members of a Masonic association cannot access Holy Communion, it aims to enlighten the conscience of the faithful about a serious consequence that they must draw from their adherence to a Masonic lodge.

The Sacred Congregation finally declares that «it is not the competence of local ecclesiastical authorities to pronounce on the nature of Masonic associations, with a judgment implying derogation from what is established above». In this regard, the text also refers to the Declaration of February 17, 1981, which already reserved to the Apostolic See any pronouncement on the nature of these associations that implied derogations from the then-current canon law (can. 2335 of the *Codex Iuris Canonici* of 1917).

Similarly, the new document, issued by the Sacred Congregation for the Doctrine of the Faith in November 1983, expresses identical intentions of reservation regarding pronouncements that would deviate from the judgment formulated here on the incompatibility of Masonic principles with the Catholic faith, on the seriousness of joining a lodge, and on the consequence that results for access to Holy Communion.

This provision indicates that, despite the diversity that may exist among Masonic obediences, especially in their declared attitude towards the Church, the Apostolic See identifies some common principles that require a similar evaluation by all ecclesiastical authorities.

In making this Declaration, the Sacred Congregation for the Doctrine of the Faith did not intend to disregard the efforts made by those who, with the proper authorization of this Dicastery, sought to establish a dialogue with representatives of Freemasonry.

However, since there was a possibility that the mistaken opinion could spread among the faithful that joining a Masonic lodge was now permissible, it considered it its duty to make them aware of the authentic thought of the Church on this matter and to warn them against an affiliation incompatible with the Catholic faith.

Only Jesus Christ is, in fact, the Master of Truth, and only in Him can Christians find the light and strength to live according to God's plan, working for the true good of their brothers.

Freemasonry and Religion

The United Grand Lodge of England is one of the oldest secular and charitable institutions globally; modern Freemasonry traces its roots to the traditions of medieval stonemasons engaged in the construction of cathedrals. Even today, the Masonic way of life is based on traditional values such as Moral Integrity, Brotherhood, Respect for others, and Charity.

Resolution of the United Grand Lodge of England in 1985[166]

- Statement Of Principle

Freemasonry is not a religion nor a substitute for a religion. It requires its members to have a full and sincere belief in a Supreme Being but does not provide its own doctrine of faith. Freemasonry is open to men of all religious faiths, and any theological discussions are prohibited during its meetings.

- The Supreme Being

The names used to denote the Supreme Being offer men of different faiths, who would otherwise remain strangers to each other, the opportunity to come together

---

[166] Declaration on Freemasonry and Religion. URL: *http://www.glri.it/dichiarazione-su-massoneria-e-religione/* (*Verified 09-18-2022*).

in the glory of the God in whom each of them believes, without the contents of invocations causing dissension among them. There is no Masonic god: a Mason's God is the God of the religion he professes. Masons gather in common respect for the Supreme Being, which remains supreme in their religious confessions. Freemasonry does not attempt in any way to merge individual religions. Therefore, there is no syncretic Masonic God.

- The Volume Of The Sacred Law

The Bible, considered by Masons as the Volume of the Sacred Law, is always kept open during Masonic meetings.

- Masonic Obligations

The obligations of Masons are always taken on the Volume of the Sacred Law or the Book they consider sacred, which is kept open. These are promises to keep the ancient modes of recognition among Masons and a commitment to follow the moral principles of Freemasonry.

- Comparison Between Freemasonry And Religion

Freemasonry lacks the fundamental elements of a religion:

a) It has no theological doctrine and, by prohibiting discussions on religion during its meetings, does not allow the emergence of a Masonic theological doctrine.

b) It does not offer sacraments and does not perform any worship.

c) It does not claim to lead to salvation through works, secret knowledge, or any other means. The reserved elements of Freemasonry concern modes of recognition along with edifying rules transferred to the symbolic, metaphorical, and moral plane and, therefore, do not concern salvation and eschatology.

- Freemasonry Supports Religion

Freemasonry is far from indifferent to religion. Indeed, without interfering with religious practices, it requires each of its members to follow their faith and place their duties towards God, whatever name is used to identify Him, above all others. The moral teachings of Freemasonry are acceptable to all religions. Freemasonry, therefore, supports religion.

Doctrinal Note on Some Questions Regarding the Participation of Catholics in Political Life[167]

The Congregation for the Doctrine of the Faith, having received the opinion of the Pontifical Council for the Laity, has decided that it would be appropriate to publish the present *Doctrinal Note on some questions regarding the participation of Catholics in political life*. This Note is directed to the Bishops of the Catholic Church and, in a particular way, to Catholic politicians and all lay members of the faithful called to participate in the political life of democratic societies.

I. A constant teaching

1. The commitment of Christians in the world has found a variety of expressions in the course of the past 2000 years. One such expression has been Christian involvement in political life: Christians, as one Early Church writer stated, «play their full role as citizens». Among the saints, the Church venerates many men and women who served God through their generous commitment to politics and government. Among these, Saint Thomas More, who was proclaimed Patron of

[167] Doctrinal Note from the Congregation for the Doctrine of the Faith, 24 November 2002

Statesmen and Politicians, gave witness by his martyrdom to «the inalienable dignity of the human conscience».

Though subjected to various forms of psychological pressure, Saint Thomas More refused to compromise, never forsaking the «constant fidelity to legitimate authority and institutions» which distinguished him; he taught by his life and his death that «man cannot be separated from God, nor politics from morality».

It is commendable that in today's democratic societies, in a climate of true freedom, everyone is made a participant in directing the body politic. Such societies call for new and fuller forms of participation in public life by Christian and non-Christian citizens alike. Indeed, all can contribute, by voting in elections for lawmakers and government officials, and in other ways to the development of political solutions and legislative choices which, as well, in their opinion, will benefit the common good. The life of a democracy could not be productive without the active, responsible and generous involvement of everyone, «albeit in a diversity and complementarity of forms, levels, tasks, and responsibilities».

By fulfilling their civic duties, «guided by a Christian conscience», in conformity with its values, the lay faithful exercise their proper task of infusing the temporal order with Christian values, all the while respecting the nature and rightful autonomy of that order, and cooperating with other citizens according to their particular competence and responsibility. The consequence of this fundamental teaching of the Second Vatican Council is that «the lay faithful are never to relinquish their participation in 'public life', that is, in the many different economic, social, legislative, administrative and cultural areas, which are intended to promote organically and institutionally the common good». This would include the promotion and defence of goods such as public order and peace, freedom and equality, respect for human life and for the environment, justice and solidarity.

The present Note does not seek to set out the entire teaching of the Church on this matter, which is summarized in its essentials in the *Catechism of the Catholic Church,* but intends only to recall some principles proper to the Christian conscience, which inspire the social and political involvement of Catholics in democratic societies. The emergence of ambiguities or questionable positions in recent times, often because of the pressure of world events, has made it necessary to clarify some important elements of Church teaching in this area.

II. Central points in the current cultural and political debate

2. Civil society today is undergoing a complex cultural process as the end of an era brings with it a time of uncertainty in the face of something new. The great strides made in our time give evidence of humanity's

progress in attaining conditions of life which are more in keeping with human dignity. The growth in the sense of responsibility towards countries still on the path of development is without doubt an important sign, illustrative of a greater sensitivity to the common good. At the same time, however, one cannot close one's eyes to the real dangers which certain tendencies in society are promoting through legislation, nor can one ignore the effects this will have on future generations.

A kind of cultural relativism exists today, evident in the conceptualization and defence of an ethical pluralism, which sanctions the decadence and disintegration of reason and the principles of the natural moral law. Furthermore, it is not unusual to hear the opinion expressed in the public sphere that such ethical pluralism is the very condition for democracy. As a result, citizens claim complete autonomy with regard to their moral choices, and lawmakers maintain that they are respecting this freedom of choice by enacting laws which ignore the principles of natural ethics and yield to ephemeral cultural and moral trends, as if every possible outlook on life were of equal value.

At the same time, the value of tolerance is disingenuously invoked when a large number of citizens, Catholics among them, are asked not to base their contribution to society and political life – through the legitimate means available to everyone in a democracy – on their particular understanding of the human person and the common good. The history of the twentieth century demonstrates that those citizens were right who recognized the falsehood of relativism, and with it, the notion that there is no moral law rooted in the nature of the human person, which must govern our understanding of man, the common good and the state.

3. Such relativism, of course, has nothing to do with the legitimate freedom of Catholic citizens to choose among the various political opinions that are compatible with faith and the natural moral law, and to select, according to their own criteria, what best corresponds to the needs of the common good. Political freedom is not - and cannot be - based upon the relativistic idea that all conceptions of the human person's good have the same value and truth, but rather, on the fact that politics are concerned with very concrete realizations of the true human and social good in given historical, geographic, economic, technological and cultural contexts. From the specificity of the task at hand and the variety of circumstances, a plurality of morally acceptable policies and solutions arises.

It is not the Church's task to set forth specific political solutions – and even less to propose a single solution as the acceptable one – to temporal questions that God has left to the free and responsible judgment of each person. It is, however, the Church's right and duty to provide a moral judgment on temporal matters when this is required by faith or the moral law. If Christians must «recognize the legitimacy of differing points of view about the organization of worldly affairs«, they are also called to reject, as injurious to democratic life, a conception of pluralism that reflects moral relativism. Democracy must be based on the true and solid foundation of non-negotiable ethical principles, which are the underpinning of life in society.

On the level of concrete political action, there can generally be a plurality of political parties in which Catholics may exercise – especially through legislative assemblies – their right and duty to contribute to the public life of their country. This arises because of the contingent nature of certain choices regarding the ordering of society, the variety of strategies available for accomplishing or guaranteeing the same fundamental value, the possibility of different interpretations of the basic principles of political theory, and the technical complexity of many political problems.

It should not be confused, however, with an ambiguous pluralism in the choice of moral principles or essential values. The legitimate plurality of temporal options is at the origin of the commitment of Catholics to politics and relates directly to Christian moral and social teaching. It is in the light of this teaching that lay Catholics must assess their participation in political life so as to be sure that it is marked by a coherent responsibility for temporal reality.

The Church recognizes that while democracy is the best expression of the direct participation of citizens in political choices, it succeeds only to the extent that it is based on a correct understanding of the human *person*. Catholic involvement in political life cannot compromise on this principle, for otherwise, the witness of the Christian faith in the world, as well as the unity and interior coherence of the faithful, would be non-existent.

The democratic structures on which the modern state is based would be quite fragile were its foundation not the centrality of the human person. It is respect for the person that makes democratic participation possible. As the Second Vatican Council teaches, «the protection of the rights of the person is, indeed, a necessary condition for citizens, individually and collectively, to play an active part in public life and administration».

4. The complex array of today's problems branches out from here, including some never faced by past generations. Scientific progress has resulted in advances that are unsettling for the consciences of men and women and call for solutions that respect ethical principles in a coherent and fundamental way. At the same time, legislative proposals are put forward which, heedless of the consequences for the existence and future of human beings with regard to the formation of culture and social behaviour, attack the very inviolability of human life.

Catholics, in this difficult situation, have the right and the duty to recall society to a deeper understanding of human life and to the responsibility of everyone in this regard. John Paul II, continuing the constant teaching of the Church, has reiterated many times that those who are directly involved in lawmaking bodies have a *«grave and clear obligation to oppose»* any law that attacks human life. For them, as for every Catholic, it is impossible to promote such laws or to vote for them.

As John Paul II has taught in his Encyclical Letter *Evangelium vitae* [168] regarding the situation in which it is not possible to overturn or completely repeal a law allowing abortion which is already in force or coming up for a vote, «an elected official, whose absolute personal opposition to procured abortion was well known, could licitly support proposals aimed at *limiting the harm* done by such a law and at lessening its negative consequences at the level of general opinion and public morality».

In this context, it must be noted also that a well-formed Christian conscience does not permit one to vote for a political program or an individual law which contradicts the fundamental contents of faith and morals. The Christian faith is an integral unity , and thus it is incoherent to isolate some particular element to the detriment of the whole of Catholic doctrine. A political commitment to a single isolated aspect of the Church's social doctrine does not exhaust one's responsibility towards the common good. Nor can a Catholic think of delegating his Christian responsibility to others; rather, the Gospel of Jesus Christ gives him this task, so that the truth about man and the world might be proclaimed and put into action.

---

[168] Evangelium Vitae (25 March 1995) – Lettera Enciclica del Sommo Pontefice Giovanni Polo II. URL: *https://www.vatican.va/content/john-paul-ii/en/encyclicals/documents/hf_jp-ii-_enc_25031995_evangelium-vitae.html* (*Verified 22/04/2022*).

When political activity comes up against moral principles that do not admit of exception, compromise or derogation, the Catholic commitment becomes more evident and laden with responsibility. In the face of *fundamental and inalienable ethical demands,* Christians must recognize that what is at stake is the essence of the moral law, which concerns the integral good of the human person. This is the case with laws concerning *abortion* and *euthanasia* (not to be confused with the decision to forgo *extraordinary treatments,* which is morally legitimate). Such laws must defend the basic right to life from conception to natural death. In the same way, it is necessary to recall the duty to respect and protect the rights of the *human embryo.*

Analogously, the *family* needs to be safeguarded and promoted, based on monogamous marriage between a man and a woman, and protected in its unity and stability in the face of modern laws on divorce: in no way can other forms of cohabitation be placed on the same level as marriage, nor can they receive legal recognition as such. The same is true the freedom of parents regarding the education of their children; it is an inalienable right recognized also by the Universal Declaration on Human Rights. In the same way, one must consider *society's protection of minors* and freedom from *modern forms of slavery* (drug abuse and prostitution, for example).

In addition, there is the right to *religious freedom* and the development of an *economy* that is at the service of the human person and of the common good, with respect for social justice, the principles of human solidarity and subsidiarity, according to which «the rights of all individuals, families, and organizations and their practical implementation must be acknowledged». Finally, the question of *peace* must be mentioned. Certain pacifistic and ideological visions tend at times to secularize the value of peace, while, in other cases, there is the problem of summary ethical judgments which forget the complexity of the issues involved. Peace is always «the work of justice and the effect of charity». It demands the absolute and radical rejection of violence and terrorism and requires a constant and vigilant commitment on the part of all political leaders.

III. Principles of Catholic doctrine on the autonomy of the temporal order and on pluralism.

5. While a plurality of methodologies reflective of different sensibilities and cultures can be legitimate in approaching such questions, no Catholic can appeal to the principle of pluralism or the autonomy of lay involvement in political life to support policies affecting the common good which that compromise or undermine fundamental ethical requirements. This is not a question of «confessional values» *per se*, because such ethical precepts are rooted in human nature itself and belong to the natural moral law. They do not require from those

who defend them the profession of the Christian faith, although the Church's teaching confirms and defends them always and everywhere as part of her service to the truth about man and about the common good of civil society. Moreover, it cannot be denied that politics must refer to principles of absolute value precisely because these are at the service of the dignity of the human person and of true human progress.

6. The appeal often made to *«the rightful autonomy of the participation of lay Catholics»* in politics needs to be clarified. Promoting the common good of society, according to one's conscience, has nothing to do with «confessionalism» or religious intolerance. For Catholic moral doctrine, the rightful autonomy of the political or civil sphere from that of religion and the Church – *but not from that of morality* – is a value that has been attained and recognized by the Catholic Church and belongs to inheritance of contemporary civilization.

John Paul II has warned many times of the dangers which follow from confusion between the religious and political spheres. «Extremely sensitive situations arise when a specifically religious norm becomes or tends to become the law of a state without due consideration for the distinction between the domains proper to religion and to political society. In practice, the identification of religious law with civil law can stifle religious freedom, even going so far as to restrict or deny other inalienable human rights».

All the faithful are well aware that specifically religious activities (such as the profession of faith, worship, administration of sacraments, theological doctrines, interchange between religious authorities and the members of religions) are outside the state's responsibility. The state must not interfere, nor in any way require or prohibit these activities, except when it is a question of public order. The recognition of civil and political rights, as well as the allocation of public services may not be made dependent upon citizens' religious convictions or activities.

The right and duty of Catholics and all citizens to seek the truth with sincerity and to promote and defend, by legitimate means, moral truths concerning society, justice, freedom, respect for human life and the other rights of the person, is something quite different. The fact that some of these truths may also be taught by the Church does not lessen the political legitimacy or the rightful «secularity[169]» of the contribution of those citizens who are committed to them, irrespective of the role that reasoned inquiry or confirmation by the Christian faith may have played in recognizing such truths.

Such «autonomy» refers first of all to the attitude of the person who respects the truths that derive from

[169] The concept can be expressed in English as both "secularity" and "autonomy." While "secularity" often pertains to the absence of religious influence, "autonomy" is a broader term referring to self-governance and independence in decision-making.

natural knowledge regarding man's life in society, even if such truths may also be taught by a specific religion, because truth is one. It would be a mistake to confuse the proper *autonomy* exercised by Catholics in political life with the claim of a principle that prescinds from the moral and social teaching of the Church.

By its interventions in this area, the Church's Magisterium does not wish to exercise political power or eliminate the freedom of opinion of Catholics regarding contingent questions. Instead, it intends – as is its proper function – to instruct and illuminate the consciences of the faithful, particularly those involved in political life, so that their actions may always serve the integral promotion of the human person and the common good.

The social doctrine of the Church is not an intrusion into the government of individual countries. It is a question of the lay Catholic's duty to be morally coherent, found within one's conscience, which is one and indivisible. «There cannot be two parallel lives in their existence: on the one hand, the so-called 'spiritual life', with its values and demands; and on the other, the so-called 'secular' life, that is, life in a family, at work, in social responsibilities, in the responsibilities of public life and in culture. The branch, engrafted to the vine which is Christ, bears its fruit in every sphere of existence and activity. In fact, every area of the lay faithful's lives, as different as they are, enters into the plan of God, who desires that these very areas be the 'places in time' where the love of Christ is revealed and realized for both the glory of the Father and service of others.

Every activity, every situation, every precise responsibility - as, for example, skill and solidarity in work, love and dedication in the family and the education of children, service to society and public life and the promotion of truth in the area of culture - are the occasions ordained by providence for a 'continuous exercise of faith, hope and charity' (*Apostolicam actuositatem*[170])». Living and acting in conformity with one's own conscience on questions of politics is not slavish acceptance of positions alien to politics or some kind of confessionalism, but rather the way in which Christians offer their concrete contribution so that, through political life, society will become more just and more consistent with the dignity of the human person.

In democratic societies, all proposals are freely discussed and examined. Those who, on the basis of respect for individual conscience, would view the moral duty of Christians to act according to their conscience as something that disqualifies them from political life, denying the legitimacy of their political involvement following from their convictions about the common good, would be guilty of a form of intolerant *secularism.* Such a position would seek to

---

[170] *Apostolicam Actuositatem,* Decreto sull'Apostolato dei Laici del Sommo pontefice Paolo VI. URL: *https://www.vatican.va/archive/hist_councils/ii_vatican_council/documents/vat-ii_decree_19651118_apostolicam-actuositatem_it.html* (*Verified 26/02/2022*).

deny not only any engagement of Christianity in public or political life, but even the possibility of natural ethics itself.

Were this the case, the road would be open to moral anarchy, which would be anything but legitimate pluralism. The oppression of the weak by the strong would be the obvious consequence. The marginalization of Christianity, moreover, would not bode well for the future of society or for consensus among peoples; indeed, it would threaten the very spiritual and cultural foundations of civilization.

IV. Considerations regarding particular aspects

7. In recent years, there have been cases within some organizations founded on Catholic principles, in which support has been given to political forces or movements with positions contrary to the moral and social teaching of the Church on fundamental ethical questions. Such activities, in contradiction to basic principles of Christian conscience, are not compatible with membership in organizations or associations which define themselves as Catholic.

Similarly, some Catholic periodicals in certain countries have expressed perspectives on political choices that have been ambiguous or incorrect, by misinterpreting the idea of the political autonomy enjoyed by Catholics and by not taking into consideration the principles mentioned above.

Faith in Jesus Christ, who is «the way, the truth, and the life» (Jn 14:6), calls Christians to exert a greater effort in building a culture which, inspired by the Gospel, will reclaim the values and contents of the Catholic Tradition. The presentation of the fruits of the spiritual, intellectual and moral heritage of Catholicism in terms understandable to modern culture is a task of great urgency today, in order, to avoid also a kind of Catholic cultural diaspora.

Furthermore, the cultural achievements and mature experience of Catholics in political life in various countries, especially since the Second World War, do not permit any kind of 'inferiority complex' in comparison with political programs which recent history has revealed to be weak or totally ruinous.

It is insufficient and reductive to think that the commitment of Catholics in society can be limited to a simple transformation of structures, because if at the basic level there is no culture capable of receiving, justifying and putting into practice positions deriving from faith and morals, the changes will always rest on a weak foundation.

Christian faith has never presumed to impose a rigid framework on social and political questions, conscious that the historical dimension requires men and women to live in imperfect situations, which are also susceptible to rapid change.

For this reason, Christians must reject political positions and activities inspired by a utopian perspective which, turning the tradition of Biblical faith into a kind of prophetic vision without God, makes ill use of religion by directing consciences towards a hope which is merely earthly and which empties or reinterprets the Christian striving towards eternal life.

At the same time, the Church teaches that authentic freedom does not exist without the truth. «Truth and freedom either go together hand in hand or together they perish in misery».

In a society in which truth is neither mentioned nor sought, every form of authentic exercise of freedom will be weakened, opening the way to libertine and individualistic distortions and undermining the protection of the good of the human person and of the entire society.

8. In this regard, it is helpful to recall a truth which today is often not perceived or formulated correctly in public opinion: the right to freedom of conscience and, in a special way, to religious freedom, taught in the Declaration *Dignitatis humanae*[171] of the Second Vatican Council, is based on the ontological dignity of the human person and not on a non-existent equality among religions or cultural systems of human creation.

Reflecting on this question, Paul VI taught that «in no way does the Council base this right to religious freedom on the fact that all religions and all teachings,

---

[171] *Dignitatis Humanae*, Declaration on Religious Liberty, released by the Sovereign Pontiff Paul VI. URL: *https://www.vatican.va/content/john-paul-ii/en/encyclicals/documents/hf_jp-ii_enc_25031995_evangelium-vitae.html* (*Verified 01/10/2022*).

including those that are erroneous, would have more or less equal value; it is based rather on the dignity of the human person, which demands that he not be subjected to external limitations which tend to constrain the conscience in its search for the true religion or in adhering to it».

The teaching on freedom of conscience and on religious freedom does not therefore contradict the condemnation of indifferentism and religious relativism by Catholic doctrine; on the contrary, it is fully in accord with it.

V. Conclusion

9. The guidelines contained in this *Note*[172] aim to shed light on one of the most important aspects of the Christian's life: the coherence between faith and life, between the gospel and culture, as recalled by the Second Vatican Council. It urges the faithful to «faithfully fulfill their earthly duties, guided by the spirit of the gospel.

Those who think they can neglect their earthly duties because we do not have a stable citizenship here but seek a future one are mistaken; they fail to realize

---

[172] The Sovereign Pontiff John Paul II, in the Audience of November 21, 2002, approved the present Note, adopted in the Plenary Session of this Congregation, and ordered its publication.

that, on the contrary, faith obliges them even more to fulfill these duties, according to each one's vocation».

May the faithful be eager «to be able to carry out all their earthly activities, unifying human, domestic, professional, scientific, and technical efforts in a single vital synthesis together with religious goods, under whose highest direction everything is coordinated to the glory of God».

+ Joseph Card. Ratzinger
Prefect

+ Tarcisio Bertone, S.D.B., Archbishop Emeritus of Vercelli
Secretary

Rome, from the Offices of the Congregation for the Doctrine of the Faith, November 24, 2002, the Solemnity of Christ the King.

Clarification from the Secretariat of State Regarding Chivalric Orders

On two occasions, namely in 1970 and in 2006[173], the Secretariat of State had to provide precise clarifications regarding congregations of faithful, present in different countries, claiming to be somehow connected to the extinct Order of the Templars.

The warning from the Secretariat of State in 1970 reads as follows:

> In recent times, and with increased insistence, the Apostolic See, both at the center, namely in the Secretariat of State, and at the periphery, namely at some Pontifical Representations, has been the object of insistence by emissaries of a certain Chivalric Order that attributes to itself the titles of Sovereign and Military of the Temple of Jerusalem.
>
> We are authorized to warn all those belonging to the Hierarchy, in Italy and abroad, reminding them that the Holy See recognizes only the Sovereign Military Order of Malta and the Equestrian Order of the Holy Sepulcher. In the specific case we are dealing with, the historical events of the ancient Order of the Temple (the Templars) are too well known, which was suppressed by Pope

[173] Delgado Galindo M., 2021, (*wk. cited*). p.21.

> Clement V (1305-1314) and was never restored by any other successor. Therefore, this modern restoration, aggravated by the claim of the name 'sovereign,' can only appear as an abuse and, therefore, illegitimate[174].

In 2006, the Secretariat, revisiting the same topic, specifies:

> In recent times, in Germany, there have been persistent rumours of an alleged recognition by the Holy See of the so-called Order of the Temple (*Templerorden*), and requests for information regarding the authenticity of a letter bearing the signature of the Eminent Cardinal Secretary of State that would endorse the claimed recognition. In this regard, we are authorized to declare that this letter is false and does not honour those who produced it[175].

The Secretariat of State, in response to frequent requests for information regarding the Holy See's stance towards Chivalric Orders dedicated to saints or having sacred titles, deems it appropriate to reaffirm the need

---

[174] Title: Secretariat of State, Note on the Sovereign Military Order of the Temple of Jerusalem Source: L'Osservatore Romano. Date: July 18, 1970, p.2.

[175] Title: Secretariat of State, Note on the Order of the Temple Source: L'Osservatore Romano Date: May 21, 2006, p.2.

to adhere to the clarification of the Vatican Secretariat of State, dated October 16, 2012172, which authoritatively states:

In addition to its own Chivalric Orders (Supreme Order of Christ, Order of the Golden Spur, Pian Order, Order of St. Gregory the Great, and Order of St. Sylvester Pope), the Holy See recognizes and protects only the Sovereign Military Order of Malta - or Sovereign Military Hospitaller Order of St. John of Jerusalem, of Rhodes, and of Malta - and the Equestrian Order of the Holy Sepulcher of Jerusalem, and does not intend to innovate on this matter.

All other Orders - whether of recent institution or derived from medieval ones - are not recognized by the Holy See, as it cannot vouch for their historical and juridical legitimacy, their purposes, and their organizational systems.

To avoid possible misunderstandings, also due to the illicit issuance of documents and the improper use of sacred places, and to prevent the continuation of abuses that then result in harm to many well-intentioned people, the Holy See confirms that it attributes no value to chivalric diplomas and their insignia issued by unrecognized societies and deems the use of churches and chapels for so-called 'investiture ceremonies' inappropriate[176].

[176] Bulletin of the Holy See Press Office, October 16, 2012.

Italian Episcopal Conference

Prot. No. 483/2012 Rome, July 3, 2012
CONFIDENTIAL NOTE

To the Most Reverend Members
of the Italian Episcopal Conference
Their Sees

Venerable Brother,

The Secretariat of State, recently communicating to this General Secretariat that it has received further reports of manifestations of Chivalric Orders held in premises owned by the Church, reiterated that «the Holy See recognizes only the Sovereign Order of Malta and the Equestrian Order of the Holy Sepulchre of Jerusalem and does not intend to renew in this regard».

While allowing me to refer to what was indicated in previous confidential notes, by the then Secretary-General H.E. Msgr. Giuseppe Beton on June 17, 2005, Prot. No. 568/05, and on July 7, 2006, Prot. No. 624/06, I take the opportunity with this letter to convey the indication to «remind those concerned of the advisability of refraining from celebrating or having celebrated in the churches and rectories of Italy ceremonies with unrecognized Orders, particularly those aimed at the so-called 'investitures' of new knights, considering also the illegality of the distribution of honours and diplomas issued by such associations in accordance with Italian laws (Articles 7 and 8 of Law No. 178, March 3, 1951, still in force).»

Thankful for your attention, I take advantage of the opportunity to offer you a fraternal greeting and confirm myself

+ Mariano Crociata
General Secretary

Essential Bibliography

Alvarado Planas J., 2019, *Templarios y Masones. Las claves de un enigma* (Templars and Masons. The Keys to an Enigma). Madrid, Spain, Editorial Sanz y Torres.

Anderson J., 2018, *Le Costituzioni dei Liberi Muratori 1723* (The Constitutions of the Free Masons 1723), Roma, Italia, BastogiLibri.

Baigent M., Leigh R., 2010, *Masones y Templarios* (Masons and Templars), Madrid, Spain, Ediciones Martinez Roca.

Bellocchi U., 1993, (edited by), *Tutte le encicliche ed i principali documenti pontifici emanati dal 1740. 250 anni di storia visti dalla Santa Sede* (All the Encyclicals and Principal Pontifical Documents issued from 1740. 250 years of history seen by the Holy See). Vol. I, Benedict XIV (1740-1758), Roma, Libreria Editrice Vaticana, pp. 289-291.

Beltrutti D., 2014, *Catechismo Templare* (Templar Catechism). Roma, Italy, BastogiLibri.

Beltrutti di San Biagio D., 2019, *Il Cavaliere del Tempio tra San Bernardo e la Libera Muratoria* (The Knight of the Temple between St. Bernard and Free Masonry), Boves, Italy, Arabafenice.

Bernard D., 2018, *Light on Masonry: A Collection of All the Most Important Documents on the Subject of Speculative Free Masonry*, Sheridan, Creative Media Partners.

Besant A., 2011, *Il Cristianesimo Esoterico* (Esoteric Christianity), Vicenza, Italia, Edizioni Teosofiche Italiane.

Biglino M., 2009, *Chiesa Romana Cattolica e Massoneria. Realmente così diverse?* (Roman Catholic Church and Freemasonry. Are They Really So Different?), Torino, Italy, Uno Editori.

Bordonove G., 2017, *Vita quotidiana dei Templari nel XIII secolo* (Daily Life of the Templars in the 13th Century), Segrate, Italia, Rizzoli.

Canavese S., 2005, *I Cavalieri Templari. Fede, Simboli e Misteri* (The Knights Templar. Faith, Symbols, and Mysteries), Aosta, Italia, Keltia Editrice.

Caprile G., 1980, *Massoneria e Chiesa Cattolica: ieri, oggi e domani* (Freemasonry and the Catholic Church: Yesterday, Today, and Tomorrow), Roma, Edizioni Paoline.

Charpentier L., 2016, *I Misteri dei Templari* (The Mysteries of the Templars), Roma, Italy, Atanòr.

Chiara inconciliabilità. Chiesa e Massoneria lo «Scandaloso» Dialogo (Clear Incompatibility. Church and Freemasonry, the 'Scandalous' Dialogue), Stamile E., Avvenire.it, November 1, 2017. URL: *https://www.avvenire*

.it/opinioni/pagine/chiesa-e-massoneria-lo-scandaloso-dialogo (*Verified 14-06-2022*).

Cipriani D., 2017, *I Cavalieri Templari. Storia, Segreti, Filosofia, Spiritualità* (The Knights Templar. History, Secrets, Philosophy, Spirituality), Roma, Italy, BastogiLibri.

Cipriani D., 2019, *Templari e Rosacroce. L'Ordine di Oriente* (Templars and Rosicrucians. The Order of the East), Roma, Italy, BastogiLibri.

Coil H. W., 1961, *Coil's Masonic Encyclopedia*, Richmond, Virginia, Macoy Publishing & Masonic Supply.

Compatibilità fra Chiesa Cattolica e Massoneria (Compatibility between the Catholic Church and Freemasonry), May 13, 2011, Lodge Giordano Bruno 40, Tables of the Brothers. URL: *https;//www. loggiagiordanobruno.com/page/24?cat=1* (*Verified 13-11-22*).

Corecco E., The Church and Freemasonry. Conference of November 4, 1994, Lugano. (*La Chiesa e la Massoneria. Conferenza del 4 novembre 1994*). URL: https://www. *eugeniocorecco.ch/scritti/scritti-pastorali/un-vescovo-e-la-sua-chiesa/ii-volume/chiesa-e-mondo-11/* (*Verified 26-06-2022*).

Dalla Gran Loggia d'Inghilterra a Bergoglio (From the Grand Lodge of England to Bergoglio), Il Decimo Toro. URL: https://www.youtube.com/watch?v=*kazyUjDE3d0* (*Verified 21-10-2022*) de la Rive A. C., 2018, *La Femme et l'Enfant dans la Franc-Maconnerie Universelle* (Woman and Child in Universal Freemasonry), London, England, Wentworth Press.

de Poncins Vicomte L., 1968, *Freemasonry and the Vatican - A struggle for recognition*. Translated from the French by Timothy Tindal-Robertson, Tooele, Utah, Eborn Books.

Delgado Galindo M., 2021, *Ordini equestri e diritto canonico. Annotazioni per un inquadramento giuridico* (Equestrian Orders and Canon Law. Annotations for a Legal Framework), Ius Ecclesiae, V. 33 N°1., Pisa, Italy, Fabrizio Serra Ed., pp. 307-331.

Demurger A., 1987, *Vita e morte dell'Ordine dei Templari* (Life and Death of the Order of the Templars), Milano, Italy, Garzanti.

Demurger A., 2006, *I Templari. Un ordine cavalleresco cristiano nel Medioevo* (The Templars. A Christian Chivalric Order in the Middle Ages), Milano, Italy, Garzanti.

Demurger A., *Cavalieri di Cristo, articolo tratto dalla rivista 'MedioEvo'* (Knights of Christ, article from the magazine 'MedioEvo'), n. 174 - July 2011. URL: *https://ora-et-labora.net/templari.html* (*Verified 06-01-23*).

Di Bernardo G., 1987, *Filosofia della Massoneria* (Philosophy of Freemasonry), Venezia, Italy, Marsilio Editori.

di Chiaravalle B. (San), 2022, *Scritti sui Templari. La regola dell'Ordine e il trattato sulla nuova cavalleria* (Writings on the Templars. The rule of the Order and the treatise on the new chivalry), Verona, Italy, Fede & Cultura.

Eliphanius, 2021, *Massoneria e Sette Segrete - La faccia occulta della storia* (Freemasonry and Secret Societies - The hidden face of history), Napoli, Italy, Edizioni Controcorrente.

Esposito F. R., 1979, *La riconciliazione tra la Chiesa e la Massoneria. Cronaca di alcuni avvenimenti e incontri* (Reconciliation between the Church and Freemasonry. Chronicle of some events and meetings), Ravenna, Italy, Longo.

Farina S., 2019, *Il Libro completo dei Riti Massonici* (The Complete Book of Masonic Rituals), Santarcangelo di Romagna, Italy, Rusconi.

Finney C. G., 1869, *The Character, Claims, and Practical Workings of Free Masonry*, Cincinnati, Ohio, Western Tract and Book Society.

Garrigou-Lagrange R., 1923, *Dieu: son existence et sa nature solution Thomiste des Antinomes Agnostiques* (God: His Existence and His Nature Thomistic Solution to Agnostic Antinomies), Paris, France, Gabriel Beauchesne, p. 725.

Grammauta F., 2013, *Templari, Massoneria e Chiese Cristiane, tra evoluzione ed etica* (Templars, Freemasonry, and Christian Churches, between evolution and ethics), Acireale, Italy, Gruppo Editoriale.

Gray D., 2020, *The Catholic Catechism on Freemasonry*, Belleville, Illinois, Saint Dominic's Media.

Graziani M., 2014, *Il Rito di York - La Massoneria Templare* (The York Rite - Templar Freemasonry), Roma, Italy, BastogiLibri.

Guasco M., *Che rapporti ci sono tra Chiesa e Massoneria* (What relations are there between the Church and Freemasonry?), Famiglia Cristiana, February 3, 2017. Maurilio Guasco. URL: *https://www.FamigliaCristiana.it/Articolo/Chiesa-e-Massoneria.aspx* (*Verified 07-09-22*).

Guénon R., 1977, *Simboli della Scienza Sacra* (Symbols of Sacred Science), Roma, Italy, Adelphi.

Guénon R., 1977, *Il Re del Mondo* (The King of the World), Roma, Italy, Adelphi.

If a Muslim is interested in becoming a Mason. Islamic Board, May 23, 2008. URL: *https://www.islamicboard.com/general/134266987-ur-muslim-becoming-nonmason.html*. (*Verified 07-07-2022*).

Il Giornale su 'Cari fratelli massoni' del cardinale Ravasi, Grande Oriente d'Italia, 17/02/2016 (Il Giornale on 'Dear Masonic Brothers' by Cardinal Ravasi, Grand Orient of Italy, February 17, 2016), URL: *https://www.grandeoriente.it/il-*

giornale-sullarticolo-cari-fratelli-massoni-del-cardinale-ravasi/ (*Verified 22-09-2022*).

La Chiesa Cattolica e la Massoneria. La Commissione per il Dialogo ha chiarito la decisiva questione (The Catholic Church and Freemasonry. The Commission for Dialogue has clarified the decisive issue), May 7, 1986, Alleanza Cattolica, Stimpfle J. URL: *https://alleanzacattolica.org/la-chiesa-cattolica-e-la-massoneria-la-commissione-per-il-dialogo-ha-chiarito-la-decisiva-questione-* (*Verified 05-12-22*).

La Chiesa & la Loggia. Il Cardinale Ravasi sul Sole 24 Ore, Cari Fratelli Massoni, 02/14/2016, G.O.I. (The Church & the Lodge. Cardinal Ravasi on Sole 24 Ore, Dear Masonic Brothers), February 14, 2016, Grand Orient of Italy. URL: *https://www.grandeoriente.it/la-chiesa-la-loggia-il-cardinale-ravasi-sul-sole-24-ore-cari-fratelli-massoni-il-dialogo-ce/* (*Verified 20-09-2022*).

La Massoneria, 1945, Firenze, pp.18-21. Documento dattilo scritto composto da 191 pagine e riservato a uso interno (Freemasonry, 1945, Florence, pp.18-21. Type written document consisting of 191 pages and reserved for internal use), URL: *https://www.corrispondenza romana.it/ naturalismo -gnosi-in-un-testo-massonico-del-rsaa/* (*Verified 07-09-2022*).

Lancianese D., 2009, *I Templari e la Massoneria* (The Templars and Freemasonry), Roma, Italy, Atanòr.

Lancianese D., 2009, *I Templari, setta esoterica. Filosofia e segreti dell'Ordine del Tempio* (The Templars, esoteric sect.

Philosophy and secrets of the Order of the Temple), Roma, Italy, Atanòr.

Lantoine A., 1937, *Lettre ou souverain Pontife* (Letter to the Sovereign Pontiff), Paris, France, Editions du Symbolisme.

Lantoine A., 1949, *Le Società Segrete attuali in Europa e in America* (Current Secret Societies in Europe and America), Roma, Italy, Edinac.

Le Forestier R., 2002, *La Massoneria Templare e Occultista* (Templar and Occult Masonry), Roma, Italy, Atanòr, vol.: I, II, III, IV.

Lennhof E., Posner O., 1952, *Internationales Freimaurerlexicon* (International Masonic Lexicon), Vienna, Austria, Amalthea Verlag.

Leone M., 2021, *Guida alle Società Segrete* (Guide to Secret Societies), Bologna, Italy, Odoya.

Lettera del Gran Maestro Bisi al Sole 24 Ore dopo l'articolo del Cardinale Ravasi su Chiesa e Massoneria, 15/02/2016, G.O.I. (Letter from the Grand Master Bisi to Sole 24 Ore after the article by Cardinal Ravasi on Church and Freemasonry, February 15, 2016, Grand Orient of Italy). URL: *https://www.grandeoriente.it/lettera-del-gran-maestro-bisi-a-il-sole-24-ore-dopo-larticolo-del-cardinale-ravasi-su-chiesa-e-massoneria/* (*Verified 20-09-2022*).

Liberi Muratori e Cavalleria (Free Masons and Chivalry), Fuocosacro, Nisticò A. URL: *http://www.fuocosacro.com*

/pagine/articoli/liberi%20muratori.htm (Verified 07-18-2022).

Llull R., 2021, *Llibre de l'Orde de Cavalleria* (Book of the Order of Chivalry), Cuneo, Italy, Araba Fenice.

Loiseleur J., 2017, *I Segreti dei Templari* (The Secrets of the Templars), Bologna, Italy, Odoya.

Lopane P., 2015, *I Templari* (The Templars), Roma, Italy, Controluce Edizioni - Nardò.

Marischi G., 2019, *Massoneria Templare e Rosacroce. Gradi cavallereschi dal XV al XXX di Rito Scozzese Antico ed Accettato* (Templar Freemasonry and Rosicrucians. Knightly degrees from XV to XXX of Ancient and Accepted Scottish Rite), Acireale, Italy, Tipheret, G.E. Bonanno.

Marziani E., 2019, *Simbologia e Ritualità Templare* (Symbolism and Rituals of the Templars), Roma, Italy, BastogiLibri.

Masala A., 2011, *All'ombra del Tempio. Notizie, curiosità e misteri sui cavalieri templari* (In the Shadow of the Temple. News, curiosities, and mysteries about the Knights Templar), Roma, Italy, Atanòr.

Massoneria e Chiesa Cattolica (Freemasonry and the Catholic Church), December 12, 1993, Avvenire, Cantoni G. URL: *http://www.corsodireligione.it/religioni/esoterismo/esoter_5b.htm (Verified 23-09-2022).*

Michelet V. E., 1985, *Il Segreto della Cavalleria* (The Secret of Chivalry), Roma, Italy, Basaia.

Mignard T. J., 1851, *Éclaircissement sur les Pratiques Occultes des Templiers* (Clarifications on the Occult Practices of the Templars), Dijon, France, Douillier.

Molle J. V., 1994, *I Templari. La regola e gli statuti dell'ordine* (The Templars. The rule and statutes of the order), Genova, Italy, ECIG.

Pellicciari A., 2020, *I Papi e la Massoneria* (The Popes and Freemasonry), Milano, Italy, Edizioni Ares.

Pernoud R., 1993, *I Templari* (The Templars), Milano, Italy, Effedieffe.

Pike A., 1927, *Morals and Dogma of the Ancient and Accepted Scottish Rite of Freemasonry*, Richmond, Virginia, Jenkins.

Pike A., 2004, *Morals and Dogma*, Whitefish, Montana, Kessinger Publishing.

Pike A., 2010, *Morals, Dogma and Clausen's Commentaries*, Foggia, Italy, Bastogi, vol. IV.

Pruneti L., 2002, *La Sinagoga di Satana. Storia dell'Antimassoneria, 1725 – 2002* (The Synagogue of Satan. History of Antimasonry, 1725 - 2002), Bari, Italy, Edizioni Giuseppe Laterza.

Reghini A., 1994, *Le Parole Sacre e di Passo dei primi tre gradi e il Massimo Mistero Massonico* (The Sacred Words and Steps of the first three degrees and the Maximum Masonic Mystery), Roma, Italy, Atanòr.

Rey D., 2017, *Peut-on Être Chrétien et Franc-Maçon?* (Can one be Christian and Freemason?), Paris, France, Salvator.

Smith Webb T., 2022, *The Freemason's Monitor, or Illustrations of Masonry*, London, England, Forgotten Books.

Steiner R., 2010, *Il Cristianesimo Esoterico e la Guida Spirituale dell'Umanità* (Esoteric Christianity and the Spiritual Guidance of Humanity), Milano, Italy, Editrice Antroposofica.

Tartaglia V., 2019, *La Religione Massonica Universale. Dio altissimo, l'ente supremo ideatore, il grande architetto creatore; l'uomo* (The Universal Masonic Religion. Highest God, the supreme creative entity, the great architect creator; man), Milano, Italy, StreetLib.

Trampus A., 2001, *La Massoneria nell'Età Moderna* (Freemasonry in the Modern Age). Bari, Italy, Editori Laterza.

Una lettrice ci domanda: si può essere cattolici e massoni? 02/07/2020 (A reader asks us: Can one be Catholic and a Mason? July 2, 07, 2020), L'Ancora online. URL: *https://www.ancoraonline.it/2020/07/02/lettrice-domanda-chiesa-massoni-compatibili* (*Verified 26-07-2022*).

Index of Names

About the Author

Diego Beltrutti di San Biagio was born in Cuneo in 1949 and currently resides there after having worked extensively in Italy and abroad as a specialized doctor.

For many years, he has been involved in Templar studies and research in the field of Chivalric Orders.

He has published the following works:

Catechismo Templare (Templar Catechism) in 2014 for the Bastogi publishing house. *Il Cavaliere del Tempio* (The Knight of the Temple) and *Il Llibre de l'Orde de Cavalleria* di Ramon Llull (The Ramon Llull's Book of the Order of Chivalry) in 2019 and 2021, respectively, for the ArabaFenice publishing house.

He curated the editions of *I Templari a Seborga* (The Templars in Seborga) in 2013 and *I Templari cuore pulsante di Seborga* (The Templars, the beating heart of Seborga) in 2019 for the ArabaFenice publishing house.

Diego Beltrutti di San Biagio currently presides over the Templar Studies Center Giorgio Carbone in Seborga.